# The glory of the Holy Land

**Cambridge University Press**

*Cambridge*
*London    New York    New Rochelle*
*Melbourne    Sydney*

# The glory of the Holy Land

## Shlomo S. Gafni /A.van der Heyden

*Page 1: Wild flowers seen throughout the Holy Land in Spring.*
*The illustrations on the title-pages are shown against the background of a sunrise at Wadi Firan in the Sinai.*
*Left-hand page, top: The Greek-Orthodox patriarch leading a procession to the Church of the Holy Sepulchre in Jerusalem.*
*Below, left: Druze priest of Jethro's shrine at Nebi Shueib in Galilee.*
*Centre: View from Tell Hazor, with the snow-crowned peak of Mount Hermon in the background.*
*Right: Old curiosity shop at Hebron selling also locally-made textiles.*
*Right-hand page, top: The Dome of the Rock as seen from the Mount of Olives in Jerusalem.*
*Right: The Coral Island in the Gulf of Eilat crowned with the remains of a Crusader castle.*

*Below left: Orthodox Jews praying at the Western Wall in Jerusalem.*
*Right: Part of the wall and bell-tower of the monastery of St. Catherine in the Sinai Peninsula.*
*Page 5, top: A Beduin woman strolls on the beach at Neviot in the Sinai Peninsula; centre: A potter's shop at Hebron; bottom: Entrance to the church at the monastery of Mar Saba.*
*Page 6, top: Entrance to the Garden Tomb at Jerusalem; centre: Taking a break to smoke a narghile in one of the numerous cafés in Jerusalem's Old City; bottom: The Church of Beatitudes overlooking the Sea of Galilee.*
*Page 7, top: Carved ornaments on the architectural fragments found at Capernaum; centre: The Greek Orthodox nuns at Nazareth have revived the delicate art of painting icons; bottom: The fortified walls of Acre.*

Design: OFRA KAMAR

Editor: YAEL LOTAN

Research: Robert D. Kaplan

Editorial Secretary: Rachel Gilon

Published by the Press Syndicate of the University of Cambridge
The Pitt Building, Trumpington Street, Cambridge CB2 1RP
32 East 57th Street, New York, NY 10022, USA
296 Beaconsfield Parade, Middle Park, Melbourne 3206, Australia

© 1978 by G.A. The Jerusalem Publishing House Ltd.,
39 Tchernechovski St., P.O. Box 7147, Jerusalem and
Shlomo S. Gafni, Jerusalem

© Cambridge University Press 1982

Library of Congress Catalogue number : 81-17054

ISBN  0 521 246121

Printed in Belgium by Offset Printing Van den Bossche

# Contents

INTRODUCTION 8

SINAI AND SANTA CATERINA 10

  The Cradle of the Faith ● The Guardians of the Burning Bush
  ● The Treasures of the Monastery Library ● God's Desert
  Fortress ● The Beduin of Santa Caterina ● The Charnel House
  and the Garden ● The Mountain of the Law

EGYPT'S ANCIENT CHRISTIANS 30

FROM THE BANKS OF THE NILE 32

OASES AND TOMBS IN THE WILDERNESS 34

  Desert Encampments and Tombs

THE TEMPLE OF HATHOR 37

MESSAGES IN THE ROCKS 38

KADESH BARNEA OF THE ISRAELITES 40

THE SYNAGOGUES AT GAZA AND MAON 41

GIANT PILLARS IN THE DESERT 42

PHARAOH'S ISLAND 45

THE WILDERNESS OF ZIN 46

NABATAEAN CITIES HALF AS OLD AS TIME 47

  Avdat ● Shivta ● Mamshit

ARAD, THE GUARDIAN OF THE FRONTIER 54

BEERSHEBA, THE CITY OF ABRAHAM 56

ASHKELON OF THE PHILISTINES 58

THE COASTLAND OF PHILISTIA 61

MYSTERIOUS CAVES AT BETH GUVRIN 62

SIDONIAN TOMBS AT MARESHA 65

ROMAN ROADS TO JERUSALEM 66

HEBRON, CITY OF THE PATRIARCHS 68

BETHLEHEM, BIRTHPLACE OF DAVID AND JESUS 70

RACHEL'S TOMB 73

BYZANTINE-PERIOD SYNAGOGUES 74

  Susia ● Eshtemoa

SOLOMON'S POOLS 77

MAR SABA IN THE JUDAEAN DESERT 78

KING HEROD'S CASTLE 81

CHESALON AND ITS MONUMENT 83

THE BIRTHPLACE OF JOHN THE BAPTIST 84

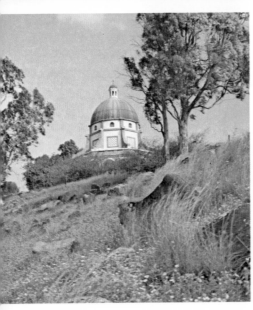

THE HOLY CITY                                                    85

    Jerusalem the Eternal • The Western Wall and Synagogues •
    Buildings and Monuments • Via Dolorosa • The Holy Se-
    pulchre and the Churches • Islam's Holy City • The Bazaar
    and the New City

BETHANY AND LAZARUS' TOMB                                       100

THE GOOD SAMARITAN                                              104

THE PLAIN OF ADUMMIM                                            105

THE DESERT SHRINE OF NEBI MUSA                                  106

WADI KELT AND ST GEORGE                                         108

QUARANTAL, THE MONASTERY OF THE FORTY DAYS                      110

JERICHO, THE WORLD'S OLDEST CITY                                112

NA'ARAN, A SYNAGOGUE IN THE DESERT                              114

THE CALIPH'S WINTER PALACE                                      116

THE SITE OF THE BAPTISM OF JESUS                                118

THE DEAD SEA SCROLLS                                            120

THE OASIS AND SYNAGOGUE AT EIN GEDI                             122

MASADA, THE LAST STRONGHOLD                                     124

    The Fortress • The Roman Camp • "Death Before Slavery"
    • Herod's Palace • The Skeletons in the Cave

THE BIBLICAL KINGDOM OF SAMARIA                                 130

SHILOH                                                          132

THE BIBLICAL CITY OF SHECHEM                                    134

JACOB'S WELL IN NABLUS                                          136

JOSEPH'S TOMB                                                   138

THE TOMB OF JOHN THE BAPTIST                                    139

THE SAMARITANS                                                  140

    Mount Gerizim • Samaritan Festivals

THE ROMAN CITY OF SEBASTIA                                      144

BETH SHEAN                                                      147

    The Amphitheatre • The Synagogue

THE SYNAGOGUE AT BETH-ALPHA                                     150

BELVOIR, THE BEAUTIFUL CASTLE                                   152

THE HEALING SPRINGS AND THE SYNAGOGUE                           154

THE RIVER AND THE LAKE                                          156

TIBERIAS AND THE SEA OF GALILEE                                 157

    The Church of St Peter • The Fishermen of the Lake • Syna-
    gogues and Tombs

THE HOME OF MARY THE MAGDALENE                                  164

THE FORTIFIED CAVES OF ARBEL                                    165

THE HORNS OF HITTIN                                             166

THE TOMB OF THE PROPHET JETHRO                                  167

THE CHURCH OF THE LOAVES AND THE FISHES                         168

THE MOUNT OF BEATITUDES                                         170

THE UMAYYAD FORTRESS AT HIRBET MINYA                            172

CAPERNAUM                                                       173

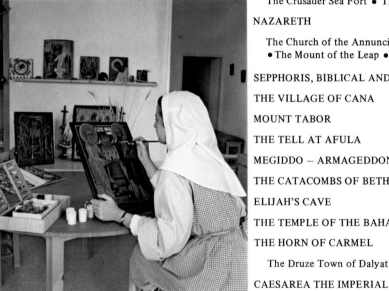

THE SYNAGOGUE OF CHORAZIN 177

THE RIVER JORDAN 178

CRUSADER CASTLES IN THE GALILEE 180

    Hunin • Qalat Namrud

THE SOURCES OF THE JORDAN 182

THE ANCIENT CITY OF HAZOR 184

MERON, CROWN OF THE GALILEE 187

    The Synagogue • The Tomb of Rabbi Simeon Bar Yohai

SAFED, A CITY OF MYSTICS 190

THE FORTRESS OF GAMLA AND THE TOWN OF PEKI'IN 194

THE SYNAGOGUE AT KEFAR BARAM 196

THE GALILEAN CITY OF KEDESH 198

THE CRUSADER CASTLES OF JUDIN AND MONTFORT 199

THE PORT CITY OF ACRE 202

    The Crusader Sea Fort • The Great Mosque • The Caravanserai

NAZARETH 206

    The Church of the Annunciation • Mary's Well • The Bazaar
    • The Mount of the Leap • The Synagogue

SEPPHORIS, BIBLICAL AND MEDIEVAL 213

THE VILLAGE OF CANA 214

MOUNT TABOR 216

THE TELL AT AFULA 218

MEGIDDO – ARMAGEDDON 219

THE CATACOMBS OF BETH SHE'ARIM 222

ELIJAH'S CAVE 225

THE TEMPLE OF THE BAHAIS 226

THE HORN OF CARMEL 227

    The Druze Town of Dalyat al Carmel • The Carmelite Monastery

CAESAREA THE IMPERIAL 231

    Strato's Tower • Herod's Roman City • Crusader Caesarea

THE FORTRESS OF ANTIPATRIS 236

THE PHILISTINE CITY AT TEL KASILLA 237

TEL AVIV 238

JAFFA, THE OLDEST PORT 240

    The Ancient Port of Joppa • Minarets and Belfries

RAMLAH, THE MOSLEM CAPITAL 246

THE SULTAN'S BRIDGE 247

GEZER OF THE HIGH PLACE 248

THE TOMBS OF THE MACCABEES 249

THE BIBLICAL VILLAGE OF EMMAUS 250

"SUN, STAND STILL OVER GIBEON" 251

LATRUN AND THE TRAPPIST MONASTERY 252

ABU GHOSH AND AQUA BELLA 254

INDEX 256

# Introduction

For hundreds of millions of people all over the world the words "the Holy Land" mean only one place. Christians, Moslems and Jews regard this land as the cradle of their respective faiths, the birthplace of the essential cultural and moral concepts by which they live.

This little country, wedged between the desert and the sea, cleft by a deep rift, ribbed with mountains, seems to contain more history than any piece of land of comparable size. Its very place names conjure up so many stories, so many dramatic events and figures; its ground is packed with remnants of the untold generations that have inhabited it continuously since the childhood of the race. What is it about this place that inspired the Ten Commandments and the Psalms, the Songs of Solomon and the thundering moral admonitions of the Prophets, the pastoral agelessness of the Book of Ruth and the spiritual anguish of Job? How did this place nurture Jesus? Could the Sermon on the Mount have been given anywhere but in the Galilee? What attracted the countless pilgrims and mystics, Crusaders and Moslem empire-builders, who between them left an incredibly varied architectural heritage?

Perhaps the time may come when scientists will be able to quantify such things as inspiration, relate them to climatic and other measurable phenomena and answer all the above questions to our descendants' satisfaction. For us it remains a mystery, and we can only wander about this country, gazing at its landscapes, breathing its air, seeing how the clear Mediterranean light fuses with the harsh glare of the desert. The traveller soon discovers that the terrain is astonishingly varied for such a small place.

As if in preparation for the human events that would take place here, a series of cataclysmic events gave the country some unique geological features. The most famous of these is the great rift valley, which runs from north to south and includes Lake Kinnereth (the Sea of Galilee), the Jordan and the Dead Sea. This is the deepest fissure in the crust of the earth, that is on dry land. To visit Tiberias on the Kinnereth, or to go to the Dead Sea, you descend hundreds of metres below sea-level. Although the rift opened millions of years ago, the most recent geological convulsion took place only eighty thousand years ago, which may be within human memory. Thus the story of Abraham and Lot and the Cities of the

Plain probably has a basis in fact. If the Sea of Galilee has a tranquil and ethereal look about it that recalls the stories of the New Testament, the Dead Sea recalls the Old Testament: "And the Lord rained upon Sodom and upon Gomorrah brimstone and fire . . .".

The rich subtropical vegetation of Ein Gedi invites associations with the Garden of Eden. Yet just behind it stretches the fierce desert, that gives no quarter to those who lose their way among its grim stony ramparts. Contrasts abound. In the Galilee the snow-capped peak of the Hermon seems to float above the warm fertile Jordan Valley, with its date-palm groves and mineral baths. Where else does a land so small offer so much to astonish and delight?

And then Jerusalem — the Holy City to much of humanity, where, within a radius of a couple of square miles, are some of the most inspiring and precious sites in the world. It is the place that David chose as the capital of his newly-founded kingdom, where Solomon built the First Temple, the place Jeremiah bewailed, Zechariah rebuilt, Herod aggrandized and adorned. It is where Jesus preached, and where the terrible events of his Passion took place. It is the place to which Mohammed first ordered his followers to address their prayers, as the Jews have done since time immemorial. It is the place where stands the third holiest Moslem shrine — the mosque of El Aqsa — and for which the Crusaders fought. On old maps Jerusalem is shown as the centre of the world: it has been that for untold numbers of devout people of the three monotheistic faiths. There is no city like it, with its strange combination of softness and hardness: the mellow tones of the stones of which it is built and on which it stands, the brilliance of its sky, the crystal purity of its air. Spreading over the hilltops, it overlooks the desert but is not part of it. It seems to stand apart, consciously unique.

We are taking you on a journey, a guided tour of the Holy Land as it looks today. Unlike the pilgrims of old, who entered the country from the north, we shall begin our pilgrimage in the south, in the footsteps of the Children of Israel as they came out of Egypt. We shall show you the landscapes and a few places you might not have discovered by yourself, and tell you something of their history. We cannot show you everything that is worth seeing — no volume would contain all that. But it will be a glimpse of the Glory of the Holy Land.

In the early 3rd century AD, years before St Anthony withdrew to the wilderness of the Egyptian desert and began the great movement of Thebaid monasticism, and more than a century before Emperor Constantine proclaimed Christianity the official religion of the Roman Empire, the first hermits settled in the Sinai desert.

In the grandeur of the harsh and majestic landscape of southern Sinai, hidden among its forbidding mountain ranges, are several oases which provided both the inaccessibility and essential needs that those mystics required to withdraw from the world. But above all it was the historical and religious associations that made the setting an ideal one for a hermitage: it was here that God revealed himself to Moses and gave his Law to the world. It was here that the Children of Israel wandered for 40 years before they were deemed fit to enter the Promised Land. And to this place flocked many early Christians, burning with mystic longing for union with God. They came from Asia Minor and Greece, the heart of the rising Byzantine Empire.

To some extent the mountains also provided a natural defence for the unarmed monks who, perched in their eyries, felt safe from marauders and armies. Nevertheless, about the middle of the 6th century, Emperor Justinian ensured their safety by having a fortified monastery built at the foot of Mount Sinai, and supplied it with a guard of soldiers as well as servants for the monks. The place also served as a military and administrative outpost of the Empire; but as time went on it became primarily a spiritual centre.

The monastery was named Santa Caterina, after St Catherine of Egypt who had been put to death by the Romans in 310. Tradition has it that her body was carried to the summit of Mount Sinai by angels, whereupon it was found by the monks and placed in a chest inside the church.

In the early days the monastery comprised a church and living quarters for the monks, with massive walls surrounding them for protection. In time more buildings were added — more chapels, accommodation for pilgrims, and a Moslem mosque. All these were built in the course of many generations and display a variety of architectural styles.

The 6th-century Byzantine historian Procopius, and Eutochius, who was Patriarch of Alexandria in the 10th century, emphasize that the monastery was built in the valley because of the proximity of the water source, and "to protect the sacred bush". These considerations overrode the strategic drawbacks.

There is also a tradition that a church was erected in the place by Queen Helena, the mother of Constantine, to whom a great many churches are ascribed in the Holy Land, but there is no evidence to support this belief.

One of the monks who lived in Santa Caterina in the 7th century, St John Climacus, was named after his famous work, *The Ladder of Divine Ascent* (ladder in Greek is *klimax*), which is a classic textbook of the ascetic and spiritual life that every Orthodox monk is supposed to read during Lent, to this very day.

Like the famous Greek Orthodox monastery on Mount Athos, Santa

Caterina belongs to no order, but remains basically a lay institution distinguished by its prophetic character and the commitment to follow faithfully the entire call of the Gospel.

The imposing walls surrounding the monastery are remarkably well preserved and typical of Byzantine architecture with their ornately carved windows. Although they were repaired and reconstructed

*1/2. Approaching Santa Caterina.*
*3. The monastery with path to Mount Sinai behind.*
*4. Byzantine cross on citadel.*
*5. Desert transportation.*
*6. Tower and chapel of St George.*

from time to time, their grace and majesty survived. The region being prone to earthquakes and tremors, reinforcements and reconstructions were unavoidable, especially after the earthquake of 1212, which caused great damage.

The four gates in the walls have served the monastery at different periods and actually tell its story. Perhaps the most interesting and certainly the most picturesque gate is the one pierced at a height of about nine metres from the ground — ingress through which was made by means of an "elevator" consisting of a strong rope and a basket. This gate was in use between the 15th and the 19th century, and provided some security. It is still in use today for hoisting in heavy supplies.

Within the compound the church is undoubtedly the most impressive building. Its exterior has remained almost intact since the Byzantine period. Its interior, however, does betray the passage of time. Built in the 6th century, it is dedicated to the Virgin Mary. An inscription nearby names Stephen of Eilat as the builder. When you enter the church, the first thing you see is the iconostasis, an enormous screen of gilded wood, spanning the width of the nave, and hung all over with icons. A Greek inscription on the iconostasis says, "This noble work was completed in Crete in August 1612, when Laurentius was archbishop and Cosmos of Crete Oikonomos of Sinai . . .". Most of the icons were painted by a certain Jeremias, a Cretan monk in the

8

9

10

11

*7. Passage between mosque and church.*
*8-10. Symbols and inscriptions connected with the site's history.*
*11. View from inside the courtyard.*

12

Sinai. Behind the screen are two silver sarcophagi, gifts of the tsars of Russia, and before the altar, under a marble canopy, rests the marble reliquary of St Catherine herself. From the canopy hang many ornamental lamps. These relics are displayed on the saint's day (25 November). The splendour of the church inspired the Greek novelist Niko Kazantzakis to exclaim, "One is stunned by the wealth . . . The walls and columns shimmer with priceless icons . . . All this gold and pearl treasure stored away in the desert for so many centuries!".

The iconostasis almost hides the monumental mosaic decoration of the apse, illustrating the Transfig-

13

uration of Christ. This work dates
from the 6th century, when the
monastery was built. Filling the
half-dome recess above the altar,
the mosaic is a work of outstand-
ing beauty. The blue halo above
the head of Christ is of a tone
almost more brilliant than the
gold background. The silver rays
spreading from the halo touch the
five figures that surround Jesus —
the Prophets Moses and Elijah,
and the Apostles John, Peter and
James. The figures of Moses and
Elijah, standing upright, are depicted in a vivid, sculptural style.
The face of Jesus is almost abstract,
characterized by the immobile,
hieratic Byzantine style. The mosaic is surrounded by 30 medal-

lions, each framing the features of
one of the apostles, evangelists or
prophets. On either side are scenes
showing Moses before the Burning
Bush and Moses with the Tablets
of the Law. Two angels with outstretched wings and the medallions of Justinian I and the Empress
Theodora appear beneath the
scene of the Transfiguration.

*12. Cedars were imported from Lebanon*
*for this 6th-century door preserved from*
*the original monastery structure.*
*Carved scenes from the Old and New*
*Testaments decorate the door.*
*13. Elaborate interior of the monastery*
*church.*
*14. One of the twelve pillars in the*
*church, each representing a month of*
*the year. Here the thirty saints of*
*November are depicted.*
*15. Close-up of the iconostasis.*

14

15

16

17

In the Greek Orthodox tradition, each day of the year has its own saint. At the Church of Santa Caterina, there are 12 columns, one for each month of the year, with rows of small icons, for all the saints of the month.

The main doors of the basilica date from the 6th or 7th century. One door depicts the Transfiguration on Mount Tabor, and the other, leading into the church from the portico, is decorated with scrolls and birds.

The monastery is a veritable treasury of ancient articles, including rare manuscripts, ritual objects and ornaments. These were donated by pilgrims on behalf of their communities, or in their own names, and by kings and princes. The result is a dazzling hodge-podge of objects ranging in age from 1,500 to 50 years old, and in styles as varied as Byzantine and rococo.

In addition to the basilica, there are several chapels. The one behind the church is the Chapel of the Burning Bush. Here, it is believed, God first appeared to Moses: "And the angel of the Lord appeared unto him in a flame of fire out of the midst of a bush, and he looked, and behold, the bush burned with fire and the bush was not consumed" (Exod. 3:2). The tiles covering the walls of this chapel are exquisite blue faience from Damascus. The floors are covered with precious rugs. A mosaic depicting the Annunciation fills the altar niche. As Kazantzakis explains, "the chapel is dedicated to the Annunciation, because the burning-but-not-consumed bush symbolizes the Virgin who received God in her body". A slab of marble marks the site of the bush that burned before Moses' eyes. Here too there is a multitude of icons covering the walls, many of them very ancient, in pure Byzantine style.

As well as this chapel, there are many others, some almost hidden from the eye. There were even more chapels in former times, as attested by the descriptions of travellers, but some of them crumbled to the ground, while others were simply torn down to make room for some other structure, more urgently needed. The ground is honeycombed with hidden chambers, most of which may not be seen by the visitor.

In the courtyard, against a chapel wall, grows a trailing raspberry bush, which is believed to have grown from the original biblical bush.

One of the first European scholars to explore the Holy Land was the German biblical critic Konstantin von Tischendorf, who in 1844 visited Santa Caterina and discovered a 4th-century Greek edition of the Bible. After many negotiations, the manuscript was finally bought from the monastery and delivered to Tischendorf's patron, Tsar Alexander II of Russia. This manuscript, known as the Codex Sinaiticus, includes the entire New Testament as well as the Books of Esther and Nehemiah, and portions of Chronicles and Jeremiah, the Epistle of Barnabas and *The Shepherd of Hermas*. It is the oldest biblical manuscript in the world, except for the Dead Sea Scrolls. (In 1933 it was sold by the Soviet Government to the British Museum.)

*16. Mosaic of the Transfiguration.*
*17. Holy altar in the Chapel of the Burning Bush.*
*18. Foliage believed by faithful to be part of the biblical "burning bush".*
*19/20. Beautiful blue tiles and a wealth of Russian miniatures and other icons grace the chapel walls.*

18

19

20

21

22

The library at Santa Caterina contains about 3,000 manuscripts, Scriptures and historical documents — many dating from the Byzantine Empire — and is one of the most precious in the world. In 1950 a British-Egyptian team catalogued the contents of the library and came across another ancient biblical manuscript, known as the Codex Syriacus, a palimpsest including an 8th-century martyrology, a 4th-century biblical script and traces of an even earlier manuscript. There is also an ancient manuscript called the Codex Arabicus, which includes biblical texts in Syriac, Greek and an Arabic translation of the Book of Job.

Fifteen centuries separated the wanderings of the Children of Israel from the arrival of the first Christian hermits who sought refuge and seclusion in the Sinai. Here, on the sacred mountain on which Moses received the Tablets of the Law, the hermits devoted themselves body and soul to the worship of God. They found inspiration in the sacred bush and

*21. The Codex Syriacus. Displayed here upside-down, it has since been uprighted.*
*22/24. Santa Caterina is famed for its library, containing numerous volumes, mostly of theological and historical content. A number of valuable manuscripts have been discovered among the library's collections.*
*23. This 6th-century representation of Christ is the oldest known hand-painted icon in the world. It is believed to have been inspired by the Holy Shroud of Edessa.*

23

24

in the remains of the martyred St Catherine, who had been tortured to death by the Romans. (In commemoration of her martyrdom, the emblem of the Order of St Catherine is a wheel with six spokes, with a sword thrust through it.) They busied themselves with building and maintaining their monastery and church, chapels, tower and courtyard — "God's desert fortress", as Kazantzakis described it. "How distant is the reeling, bellowing world!" he exclaimed after spending a few days in Santa Caterina. And, although nowadays there is a constant stream of visitors (except in winter, when the little community is all but cut off from the world by snow and inclement weather), there is still about it an atmosphere of perfect spirituality.

For those who wish to study the history of Santa Caterina, the myriad inscriptions found everywhere — on the stones, wooden doors and panels, furniture and beams, and on the plastered walls — are of great value. Reliable information about the early phases of the history of the monastery is scarce. The earliest source that describes the place and its founding is the Greek Eutychius, who wrote four centuries after the event. The inscriptions, therefore, are of great significance. Of the 200 or so which have been deciphered and identified, 16 — all of them Greek — appear to date from the period between AD 500 and 700. Some of the oldest ones, carved into the roof beams in the basilica, date from 548 to 565. (This is deduced from the fact that they mention Emperor Justinian as living and his wife Theodora as dead.) Another inscription, mentioning the name of the abbot in whose lifetime it was written, dates it as no later than 600.

These early inscriptions yield much more than bare information about the date of certain structures and art works in Santa Caterina. Much can be gleaned from them about the cultural world of the early monks. Analysis of the spelling and style of writing and various references made show that the monks who lived here in the early centuries of the Middle Ages were Nabataeans, Armenians and Syrians, as well as Greeks. Their world was that of the Near East, and they knew of nothing beyond it. Later inscriptions include those of the Crusaders.

The refectory of Santa Caterina adjoins the southwest corner of the basilica. Like other refectories in Greek Orthodox monasteries, this elongated, vaulted dining-room

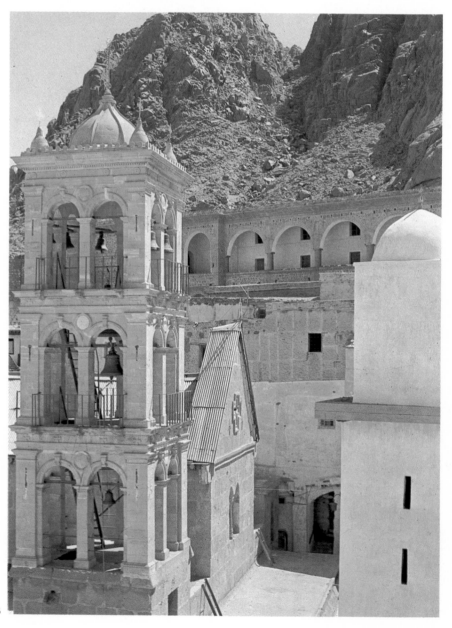

*25/26. Bell tower built by the Russian Tsar, Alexander, in 1871 — the 11th-century mosque stands to its right. The view from inside the tower is of the oldest section of the monastery.*

25

27

28

29

of the monks is decorated with a mural of The Last Supper. The fresco here dates from 1573, and it faces the entrance door.

Nowadays there are 25 monks at the monastery, most of them Egyptian-born Greeks. This figure has remained more or less constant for the past century. Before that it fluctuated a great deal, with as many as 400 in the first half of the 14th century, and a mere two at the beginning of the 17th.

At Santa Caterina the monks live according to the rule of St Basil. They eat no meat at all, but are allowed fish, which is sometimes brought up from the coast. On rare occasions they drink an alcoholic beverage called *raki*, made from dates. During the many ritual fasts, they do not eat any food originating from animals, including milk and eggs.

The day begins with the tolling of the bell, as many strokes as the numbers of years Jesus lived on earth. A piece of wood suspended from the ceiling — called a *symandra* — is struck with a wooden mallet to summon the brothers to early morning prayers in the basilica. The monk's day is spent in prayers, work in the workshops and the library, and attending to the tourists and pilgrims. This simple routine has not varied for many centuries. There is a legend that the Prophet Mohammed visited the monastery of Santa Caterina and enjoyed its hospitality.

The Crusader inscriptions are to be found in the refectory, where they were carved with some elaboration, often including the sign of the cross, a coat of arms or a coronet. These proud knights, who had ridden all the way from Western Europe to wrest the

30

31

Holy Sepulchre from the Moslems, swept down to the Sinai with all their superb panoply, to be received into the Order of Santa Caterina. Only one who was already a knight of the Order of the Holy Sepulchre could seek this honour. The emblem of the Order of St Catherine was a spoked wheel with a sword through it. It seems that admission into this order was neither simple nor cheap. A medieval German proverb about the various knightly orders says, "That of the Holy Sepulchre — the noblest; that of St. Catherine — the costliest . . .". It is likely that some of the fine medieval treasures at Santa Caterina were in fact donated by the Frankish knights and barons who sought to be received into the Order of St Catherine. Nowadays, only their inscriptions remain to connect them with this desert retreat.

There is something touching and incongruous about these traces of the age of chivalry and splendour in the midst of the bare, whitewashed simplicity of a desert monastery. So much fanfare and gorgeous display, so much physical courage and ambition, such pride of birth and earthly position! Yet what survives is the wind-scoured mountainside, the routine of the monks, and the desert sunlight on the bare walls and the russet roofs of the monastery.

The monastery on Mount Sinai is no longer a fortress defending a helpless community of monks from nomadic marauders prowling through the wilderness. For many years now the monks have lived in peaceful coexistence with the neighbouring Beduin tribesmen, from whom they buy fish and produce, and who work as the servants at the monastery. For, despite its harsh and inhospitable nature, the Sinai peninsula has for untold generations been home to nomadic tribes who have learned to live by its rigid laws.

The 10,000 or so Beduin of the Sinai peninsula belong to the tribes of the Towara group, and are divided into seven large clans. They have been roaming the desert for centuries, and have made their living by cultivating the small strips of arable land around the oases, by breeding sheep and

*27-29. Guest-house at the monastery, reserved for important visitors. In the top photograph the archbishop's private apartments are visible on the left.*
*30-32. Crusader carvings on the monastery walls, representing the names and weapons of the knights.*

33

camels or by fishing in the northern lake area and off the coast. Their way of life has hardly changed through the millennia — the camel provides them with the wool for their cloaks, with milk and sometimes meat, as well as transportation; the goats and sheep also provide wool for clothes and tents, as well as being a source of food; the palm trees provide dates. Coffee, tea and sugar are purchased in the towns, or traded for their own home-made goods.

34

35

The Beduin man wraps himself in a heavy, black cloak called an *abayah,* and his head with a white cloth which is held in place by a black cord. The women are often tattooed, and wear veils fringed with silver coins. Their dresses are black, often ornamented with exquisite embroidery. Small children often run around naked. Beduin festivities are celebrated with a great and lavish spread — a whole sheep is roasted, mounds of fluffy rice crowned with fried pine nuts, strong tea and sweet black coffee flow freely. The Beduin, being devout Moslems, drink no alcoholic beverages. They are a courtly, hospitable people, with a strong sense of tradition and propriety. To live among them is to experience the way of life of the biblical patriarchs, and to understand the tales of the Old Testament so much better. As Abraham welcomed the three messengers of God, and had the fatted calf slaughtered to provide a feast for them; as Isaac travelled in a leisurely manner from oasis to oasis, his family subsisting on its cattle and the occasional hunt; as Jacob herded the sheep of his father-in-law Laban, whose daughters Leah and Rachel he took to wife after extensive bargaining — so do these desert inhabitants live to this day.

As Santa Caterina the Beduin servants do most of the household chores, from cooking to washing and cleaning. They also provide some protection for the monks, and are often their principal links with the outside world. In the midst of this devout Christian community, the Beduin continue their own Moslem customs and traditional way of life.

36

Caravans come and go, the camels swaying slowly down the timeless desert routes, as they have since time immemorial. The rhythm of the desert is in the blood of its inhabitants, and the ancient *modus vivendi* of hermits and nomads goes on, and no doubt will go on, for hundreds of years to come.

33. *Beduin children in the Sinai.*
34. *A Beduin servant takes time out to pray.*
35. *Beduin and camel on the path leading to Mount Sinai.*
36. *Here, in the oldest section of the monastery, laundry is hand-washed by Beduin servants to this very day.*
37. *A group of Beduin at Santa Caterina engrossed in a game of backgammon.*

37

38

39

40

The mystical view that Man's life on earth is insignificant and worthless is illustrated by the collection of skulls and bones of countless monks who lived and died at Santa Caterina. This gruesome collection is kept in one of the chapels outside the monastery walls. Traditionally, a body is buried in the ground for a period of two years, and then dug up. The skull is then severed from the skeleton, and placed in a special chamber with the others. The Greek Orthodox believe that the head is the most important part of the body during life, and the skull is also an effective reminder of the inevitable end that awaits us all. The bones, too, are kept, but in an indistinguishable heap. The skulls of famous monks are kept on display in special niches, with tags to identify them. One monk whose remains are intact, and displayed draped in his original clothes, is Stephen of Eilat. Besides being the builder of the church, he is believed to have been the monastery's gate-keeper, whose business it was to question visitors and verify their worthiness to enter the holy premises. Clad in a purple cowl and cloak, the skeleton of St Stephen guards the two vaulted rooms where all the bones are kept.

By contrast, the garden and orchard outside the monastery provide a relaxing, sunny retreat. Here the visitor can enjoy the perfect peace that comes in such a setting — the ancient olive trees, the mellow tones of the rocks and stones, the sighing of the wind and the muffled sounds from the monastery. From here you can see the towering peaks of the south Sinai range, one of which is Mount Sinai itself — called *Jebel Musa* in Arabic and *Har Moshe* in Hebrew, meaning the Mountain of Moses. At 2,260 metres above sea-level, it is not the tallest peak of the range — Mount St Catherine is higher — but it is the most sacred.

The climb up Mount Sinai is not a difficult one. It is 700 metres from the monastery to the summit. There is a cypress tree just below the summit and two small chapels beside it. One is said to stand on the very spot where Elijah heard the "still small voice" (I Kgs. 19:11-12).

The path leading up to the summit
is straightforward. The descent is
usually made down another path,
consisting of 3,000 steps, known
as *Sidna Musa* (Master Moses).

Having reached the summit, the
view that spreads before your eyes
is the most dramatic and awe-
inspiring in the world. Sinai: the
childhood of the human race lies
along these gaunt and magnificent
peaks that look up at the immacu-
late sky. Here the Law was given
to the Children of Israel, who
would wander in this wilderness
for 40 years before entering the
Promised Land, leaving the bones
of their leader and prophet on the
threshold. The spirit of the Old
Testament hovers here, like a
thunderbolt about to strike, or
like a mystic fragrance from ancient times. Sinai: the stony barrier
between Asia and Africa, the land-
bridge connecting the civilizations
of the Nile Valley and Mesopotamia, a triangle of mountains and
oases, of sand-storms and blizzards,
of God-obsessed inhabitants under
a burning sky.

41

*38. Countless skulls of monks are dis-
played in a chapel outside the monastery
walls.*
*39. The remains of archbishops are en-
closed in screened recesses.*
*40. Outside the gruesome skullroom
one finds the sunny monastery garden
retreat.*
*41. This archway is known as St
Stephen's gate, for it is believed that
the famous monk sat on this very spot
and heard confessions of pilgrims visiting
the monastery and its surroundings. St
Stephen died in AD 580 and his skeleton
is displayed intact in the skullroom.*
*42. View from the summit of Mount
Sinai with the higher slopes of Mount
St Catherine in the background. The
inscriptions in the rock date from 1850.*
*43. (overleaf) Panoramic view from atop
Mount Sinai. Ras Afafa, the lowest rock
on the Sinai slopes, is seen in the foreground.*

42

44

The Coptic Christians of Egypt are a living remnant of the Nile country's ancient past. The community traces its origins to the very first Christian converts in that country. The language of the Coptic liturgy is that of the Pharaohs. In fact, the word Copt, which in Arabic is *qubt*, derives from the Greek *aigyptos*, meaning "Egyptian". In the Middle Ages, when Moslem Egyptians no longer called themselves by that name, Copt came to signify the Christians of Egypt.

Coptic art and ritual help to reconstruct early Christianity, for no other Christian community has so faithfully preserved its ancient forms. Unlike Byzantine-Greek art, Coptic art has never been bound to strict, traditional forms and shows how pagan motifs were adopted by the followers of Jesus in Roman Egypt. Column capitals are often decorated with wreaths, birds and animals. Their sculpture and textiles often include representations of Greek gods.

Coptic churches are a combination of Byzantine and Roman-basilican forms. The interiors of the churches of Old Cairo are veritable museums of ancient iconography and furniture. The lavish use of green, brown and dark orange colours give the icons a naturalistic quality enhanced by the naïve quality of the drawing. The furniture is often inlaid with ivory, and the area of the altar is usually rich in lattice work.

The Coptic language is basically the vernacular of ancient Egypt, written, however, in the Greek alphabet. It served the need to bring to the common people the Greek translation of the Bible in the first centuries after Jesus. It is no longer a spoken language, but survives in the church liturgy, and coptic literature consists mainly of religious writings.

Coptic culture is rich not only in religious doctrine, language and

45

46

art, but in legends as well. The lives of the Coptic saints offer insights into the culture of a people who shroud their origins in myth, much like the ancient Greeks. For example, the tale of the founding of the town of Mareotis: no one knew where St. Mari Mina was buried, until a shepherd saw one of his sheep, which was diseased, rolling itself dry in the sand after bathing, and miraculously its sores were healed. The shepherd now took all his flock to that spot, and the sheep that were sick were all healed as well. The king heard this story and sent his daughter, who was stricken with leprosy, to the same place. She too rolled in the sand and was cured. Next, the saint appeared to the king's daughter in a vision and told her to dig under the miracle-working sand. This she did, and Mari Mina's body was discovered. A church was built on the site, around which grew the town of Mareotis.

More than any other Christian denomination, the Copts are associated with the advent of the monastic movement. St. Anthony, the first monk who followed the footsteps of Elijah and Jesus, was an Egyptian. A Coptic monastery still stands in the eastern desert near the Red Sea where the saint spent the last years of his life. In the early centuries of the church, Coptic chapels and monasteries dotted the banks of the Nile as far south as Ethiopia. Now only a few are left. There are two clusters of desert monasteries, one near the Red Sea and one in the western desert between Cairo and Alexandria. West of Aswan are the ruins of the famous 8th-century compound of St. Simeon; here the frescoes and icons have been stripped off the walls and only the bare structure of the monastery remains.

According to most statistical estimates, there are about seven million Copts in Egypt. They have a chapel at the Church of the Holy Sepulchre in Jerusalem. A highly distinctive community, with characteristic features, they are a living vestige of biblical times.

*44. Carvings on the lintel of the Coptic "White Monastery" near Sohâq by the Nile, built in the 4th century.*
*45. Interior of one of the chapels.*
*46. A Coptic monk.*
*47. Traditional crafts are still plied by the Copts.*

47

The greatest of the Old Testament stories — that of the Exodus of the Children of Israel from Egypt after 400 years of bondage — began on the banks of the Nile.

The Hebrew infant, Moses, was placed by his mother in "an ark of bulrushes", which she "daubed ... with slime and with pitch, and put the child therein and she laid it in the flags by the river's brink" (Exod. 2:2-3). For Pharaoh had decreed that all male Hebrew children were to be put to death. Discovered by Pharaoh's daughter, he was brought up in the royal household, but his sense of jus-

tice made him emerge as the leader of the Children of Israel out of the land of bondage towards the Promised Land.

The Nile has not changed since those far-off times. Boats such as Moses might have seen still ply its length, and the pyramids stand in eternal silence, dominating the scene.

*48/50. The earliest pilgrims must have often passed by the Pyramids and crossed the Nile River on their way to the Holy Land.*
*49. The church at A-Tor was built at an important landing point on the Red Sea, and pilgrims could stay at its hostels.*

'49

48

50

51

52

53

The Sinai desert is one of the most rugged areas in the world, with jagged rocks, towering mountains and deep gorges running off towards the sea which surrounds the peninsula. One of these gorges is Wadi Firan (biblical Paran). It begins below Mount Sinai, where it collects the rainwater that runs off the sides of the mountain, and continues northwest to the Gulf of Suez. The route along this wadi has been called one of the most spectacular in the world. The 19th-century English writer and explorer, Richard Burton (of *A Thousand and One Nights* fame), described this route as one that can be travelled "till near sunset in the wilderness without ennui".

The upper part of Wadi Firan, not far from the monastery of Santa Caterina, is also called Wadi al Sheikh. It is the place where the Moslem prophet Nebi Salah is buried, in a small square tomb surrounded by many whitewashed Beduin graves. He was a 7th-century Moslem man of religion, whom tradition describes as a companion of the Prophet Mohammed. The local Beduin consider themselves his descendants.

Some 60 kilometres further west, about halfway along the wadi, is the Firan Oasis. It is 8.5 kilometres long and 200 metres wide, and appears like a vision of paradise to the weary desert traveller. There are hundreds of date palms, and in their blessed shade grow flowers and shrubs. The oasis has been identified with Rephidim, where Moses brought forth water from the rocks (Exod. 17:1-6). The day after this miracle was wrought, the Children of Israel had to fight the Amalekites in Rephidim, a battle in which the fortunes of the

Israelites rose or fell according to whether Moses' arms were raised or lowered.

In the early centuries of this era, the wadi attracted many Christian monks who established their hermitages in this area, especially around the Firan Oasis, which is the largest oasis in the Sinai desert. Surrounded by majestic mountains, with the palm trees to provide essential sustenance, and the singing of the birds, their retreat must have been inspiring.

51. *Sunrise in Wadi Firan.*
52. *The Firan Oasis.*
53. *Greek Orthodox monastery.*
54. *Byzantine chapel overlooking wadi.*
55. *5,000 year-old stone structures.*

54

55

56

The desert dwellers know no borders and move about the wilderness with the seasons in search of pasture for their flocks. But this is not to say that there are no fixed locales to which they are attached.

Some places are sanctified by tradition, usually because they mark the burial place of a saintly person, or of the traditional ancestor of the tribe.

These places serve as sites for regular gatherings of the clans belonging to the tribe. Here they forgather and hold feasts and celebrations in honour of the saint or ancestor, and here they hold their tribal courts, and conclude agreements and betrothals.

Most of the tombs are simple structures, generally domed, made of stones, mud and plaster, the roof generally being whitewashed, so that it can be seen from far away. These landmarks give the otherwise grim and impersonal wasteland its human dimension, which seems as much a part of the scenery as the rocks.

It takes hours of hiking and mountain-climbing to reach the remote temple of Hathor in southwestern Sinai. The Beduin have given it the name *Serabit el-Khadem* (Pillars of the Slaves), due to the many hieroglyphics on its columns, which describe the beating of a Semitic slave by an Egyptian official. This region of the Sinai desert was a source of turquoise and copper mining in the 4th millennium BC, and the temple was then built in honour of the Egyptian goddess Hathor. the quarries were abandoned in the 12th century BC, but since then Beduin have sifted the sands surrounding the temple in hopes of uncovering the blue-green

57

58

stones. One of the most interesting
finds in this site was a small statue
containing a pictographic inscription, an example of the earliest
known Semitic alphabet.

59

*56. Tomb of Nebi Salah — the prophet
Salah — in the Sinai.*
*57. Beduin encampment in Wadi Firan.*
*58. A Beduin family near Wadi Sidri.*
*59. A granite head of the Egyptian
goddess Hathor at Serabit el Khadem.*
*60. The site of Serabit el Khadem.*

60

The roads of the Negev and Sinai, linking Africa and Asia, have been traversed by pilgrims for centuries. Stone markings found along these routes bear testimony to the vast numbers of passing travellers. One valley in particular, in the southern Negev, contains so many markings that it has come to be known as the Valley of the Inscriptions.

These etchings, on white stone, were first discovered by Christian pilgrims in Roman-Byzantine times. They include Egyptian hieroglyphics, Jewish religious symbols (*menorahs*), as well as messages, prayers and blessings, often of minor significance, in Greek, Latin, Aramaic and Hebrew. The Nabataeans were an early Arabian people who had an independent kingdom in the Hellenistic period. Their dealings with merchants and soldiers, who passed along this route on their travels between the copper mines of the Negev and the port of Eilat, were largely responsible for the spread of the Aramaic language and hence the number of inscriptions in that tongue.)

Many inscriptions date from the 2nd and 3rd centuries AD, but some are much older and can be traced to the time of the Exodus from Egypt. Indeed, the wandering Hebrews, led by Moses, are said to have passed along this route. The fact that many of the etchings are found off the main road seems to indicate that they were made not by travellers but by the desert dwellers.

*61. Egyptian inscriptions on rocks near ancient coppermines.*
*62. Nabataean inscriptions near Eilat.*
*63/64. Rock pictures in Wadi Firan.*
*65. Menorah carved in rock wall.*
*66. Greek inscription above and Hebrew inscription with menorah below.*
*67. Nabataean carvings in Wadi Firan.*

61

62

63

64

65

66

67

This oasis on the border between the Sinai and the Negev has been held sacred since time immemorial, as its name shows — *Kadesh* meaning "holy" in Hebrew and other Semitic tongues. The patriarch Abraham resided there (Gen. 20:1). It was also called En-Mishpat, meaning the Spring of Judgment, (Gen. 14:7), which suggests that it might have been a centre for tribal justice.

However, it is with Moses and his family that the place is most frequently associated in the Old Testament. It was here that Miriam, Moses' sister, died and was buried (Num. 20:1); here Moses struck the rock with his rod and made water come out abundantly for the thirsting Israelites (*ibid.* 20:11). After these events Moses sent messengers to the king of Edom, asking that the Children of Israel be permitted to pass through his kingdom on their way to the Promised Land: "Behold, we are in Kadesh, a city in the uttermost of thy border," (*ibid.* 20:14-17).

The name Kadesh has been pre-served, but somewhat east of the biblical site, where a spring is known by the name of Ein al Kudeis. The tell which marks the true site of the ancient Kadesh is called Ein al Kudeirat, and represents the last of a series of strongholds that guarded the southwestern frontier of the Holy Land. Remains of an Israelite fortress, dating from the Judaean kingdom, were uncovered here; it includes a casemate wall with towers. Roman and Byzantine remains were also found here.

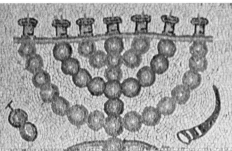

The ancient Jewish synagogue of Gaza was discovered near the harbour, which was in Byzantine times called Neapolis, the new city. An inscription shows that the building was erected in 508-9 A.D., and was donated by two brothers, timber merchants, named Menachem and Jesse. A particularly striking part of the mosaic floor shows an Orpheus-like King David, in Byzantine robes, playing the harp. Traditional Jewish symbols depicted in relief on a column of Gaza's Great Mosque — a ram's horn, a palm front and a *menorah* — suggest that the Jewish population of Talmudic-era Gaza was considerable. Under Arab rule in medieval times, the Jews of Gaza continued to flourish. The arrival of the Crusaders put an end to Jewish life in Gaza.

Remains of the Canaanite and Philistine city of Gaza were found at the nearby Tell al-Ajul. The later period is associated with the exploits of Samson, who brought down the temple of Dagon. According to legend, he is buried beneath the Great Mosque.

The southwest of the Holy Land is noted for mosaic floors from the Byzantine period. Not far from Gaza, a resplendent floor was uncovered in the fields of kibbutz Nirim. It had decorated the 6th century synagogue at Maon, and is remarkable for its resemblance to the floor of a Byzantine church discovered not far from here, but with the addition of several traditional Jewish symbols near the apse, notably, a *menorah* flanked by two lions.

*68. The oasis at Kadesh Barnea was an important way station in biblical times.*
*69. Mosaic decoration at the synagogue of Maon.*
*70. Detail from the synagogue floor at Gaza, depicting King David playing the harp.*

71

71. *"Solomon's Pillars" near the Timna copper mines.*
72. *Camel with Beduin saddlebags.*
73. *Corner formation near "Solomon's Pillars".*
74. *The gigantic "Amram Pillars".*

72

73

76

A few miles south of Eilat a small island rises out of the brillant blue sea, a mere 270 metres from the shore. It is tawny and bare, and so is the fortress that seems to grow naturally on its humped spine.

This little rock, which tourists have mistakenly dubbed the Coral Island, is called *Gesirath Faraun*, meaning Pharaoh's Island in Arabic. A mere 320 metres long and 160 metres wide, it is associated with some of the greatest names in the history of the Middle East. Its Arabic name hints at the fact that, at the time of Rameses III, Egyptian ships used to moor here on their way to and from Eilat, where they were loaded with copper from the Timna mines. The remains of a low wall surrounding the island date back to the Israelite era. "And King Solomon made a navy of ships in Ezion-Geber, which is beside Eloth, on the shore of the Red Sea, in the land of Edom ... Once in three years came the navy of Tharshish, bringing gold, and silver, ivory, apes and peacocks" (I Kgs. 9:26, 10:22).

These evocative words are easily recalled when one views the Coral Island. It is very likely that the light, Phoenician-style vessels of Solomon's navy and that of his ally, Hiram, King of Tyre, docked here, on their way to East Africa and India.

King Baldwin of the Crusader Kingdom of Jerusalem built a fort on the island to guard the access to the strategically-vital harbour; but it was Saladin, the gallant Saracen conqueror, who built the fortress that crowns the island. Nowadays the austerely beautiful island attracts skin divers, who come from all over the world to enjoy the spectacular tropical underwater flora and fauna of this breathtaking bay.

*75. Wadi Sidri in the Negev.*
*76. Coral Island in the bay of Eilat.*
*A fortress wall can be seen.*

77

The desert of Zin is mentioned several times in the Old Testament. It was in this frightful wilderness that Miriam, Moses' older sister, died and was buried. It was here, too, that the Israelites, maddened by thirst and fear, rebelled against their leaders, Moses and Aaron, and demanded to be taken back to Egypt. Then "Moses lifted up his hand, and with his rod smote the rock twice: and water came out abundantly, and the congregation drank, and their beasts also" (Num. 20:11).

78

79

The Nabataeans are something of
a mystery, even in the chequered
history of the Holy Land. It is not
known where they came from, or
how they disappeared. Between
the 4th century BC and the 2nd
century AD these semi-nomadic,
gifted and adaptable people settled
in Edom in Transjordan and in
the Negev. Their language was
Aramaic, which was more or less
the *lingua franca* of the region,
and they were sometimes described
as Arabs. Their religion was pagan-
oriental, but with an overlay of
Hellenistic influences, which are
also found in their art.

During the wars of the Hasmonaeans against the Seleucid Hellenist kingdom of Syria, the Nabataeans offered the Jewish priests
and warriors help and refuge. Later,
the Nabataean expansion and that
of the kingdom of Judaea inevitab-
ly clashed, with the result that
when Pompey marched on the
Holy Land he was able to defeat

80

81

*77. Canyon in the Zin desert.*
*78. Beduin women tend their camels in*
*the desert.*
*79. Stone carvings on the lintel at the*
*entrance of a house at Shivta.*
*80/81. Ruins of a Byzantine church*
*at Shivta.*

82

83

84

both small nations with much less effort.

Under Roman rule the Nabataeans enjoyed a measure of autonomy, and lived undisturbed in their desert cities. The most famous of these was Petra, "the rose-red city half as old as time", where the Jewish high priest Jason was given asylum by the Nabataean ruler Aretas during the revolt of the Maccabees. It is a magnificent site to this day, carved entirely out of the living rock ("Petra", meaning rock, is the Greek form of *Selah*, named in II Kings 14:7 as an Edomite town.)

But what distinguished the Nabataeans even more than Petra, more than their renown as pioneer traders along the spice route from India, and more than their attractive, oriental-Hellenistic art, were their agricultural achievements. These nomadic people, wherever they came from, came to terms with the desert and the harsh living conditions of the rainless plains better than anyone in history. In their centres at Avdat (also known as Obodah) and Shivta in the Negev, they left traces of extremely sophisticated engineering methods, by which they were able to collect the scant rainfall so efficiently as to have enough water for extensive cultivation. Today an experimental agricultural farm in the Negev has reconstructed the Nabataean systems and has produced ample crops, showing that the ingenuity of the ancients still has much to teach us, even in this era of super-technology. Indeed, at a time when problems of energy and depleting resources beset the world, the ingenuity of the Nabataeans may be emulated by modern countries with similar problems.

Avdat, which was a caravan station between Petra in Transjordan and Gaza on the Mediterranean, was founded about 400 BC, and named after the Nabataean king. In the 1st century BC it was built up and greatly developed by King Aretas IV. Some 50 years after the birth of Jesus, Avdat was sacked by desert nomads, but revived under the rule of the last Nabataean king, Rabel II. Though no doubt it still served as a trading post for caravans, Avdat had been subsisting on agriculture for the last 200 years. The site was temporarily abandoned, but inhabited again in the 3rd century AD, evidently by descendants of the original Nabataeans. Some historians believe that this was a result of Roman concern about the southern frontier. Another reason might have been the renewed efforts to mine copper in the Sinai desert, with the consequent need for urban centres in the vicinity. However, by the time the Persians invaded the Holy Land in the early 7th century, Avdat was all but abandoned. It was finally destroyed by the conquering Arab armies in 636.

The archaeological site at Avdat is a spectacular plateau on top of a stony hill, overlooking the vast plains of the central Aravah. The colours of the desert predominate: the colour of lions and gazelles, camels and sheep. The sunsets here are dazzling long displays of orange and red-gold skyscapes.

85

*82. Cross carved in stone wall of the St George Church at Shivta.*
*83. View from above of cross-shaped structure in church baptistery.*
*84. Remains found at Shivta — the hole in the centre is for tying horses.*
*85. A general view of the site at Avdat.*
*86. Stone archway at Avdat site.*

86

A workshop uncovered here revealed the beautiful fine ceramic-ware of the Nabataeans. The most impressive structure found at the site was a building complex, including a Nabataean temple and two Byzantine churches dating from the 4th and 5th centuries AD.

Shivta (also called Sobata) lies west of Avdat. Located some distance from the caravan route, it was always a farming community. Its natural situation is less spectacular than Avdat's, nor was its history as dramatic. Less fortified than Avdat, this peaceful and prosperous town was spared by the conquerors, who preferred to avail themselves of the rich produce rather than destroy its source.

Archaeological exploration at Shivta shows that it was founded at the end of the 1st century BC, just before the birth of Christ. This was the time when Nabataean agriculture was at its peak, and Shivta was surrounded by a series of channels which led the scant rainwater and the dew that falls in the night down the gentle slopes to the fields below. The place must have looked so peaceful and unthreatening, that the Romans were Shivta's best customers.

87

88

In the 5th century the Byzantine rulers of the Holy Land repopulated the city, and by the 6th century there were three churches in Shivta. There was also a monastery attached to the largest church, in the northern part of the city. It was a lavishly-endowed city, with marble halls and paved streets, cisterns and sewage. Thanks to the desert climate, Byzantine Shivta was perfectly well preserved, and its municipal form is as clearly seen as Pompeii's.

It seems that the Arabs also spared Shivta, which had no walls or ramparts to defend it. Apparently the only change they made was the addition of a small mosque within the compound of the south church, without interfering with the existing structure. Only this, and a few pieces of pottery, remain to attest to the presence of Arabs in Shivta in the 7th century. Nevertheless, in the 8th century the city was abandoned. The desert winds blew sand over it, and before long it was entirely forgotten, like the other Nabataean cities of the Negev. Only in the 19th century, when European travellers first began to take an interest in the archaeology of the Holy Land, did the elusive and intriguing Nabataean culture begin to be discovered.

*87. Spring flowers bloom even in the semi-arid Negev.*
*88. This Byzantine structure, which apparently functioned as living quarters, is found at the foot of the acropolis at Avdat below the remains of the southern church. It dates from the 6th or 7th century AD.*
*89. An upturned mill wheel lies on the ground before the walls and gate that once protected Byzantine Avdat.*
*90. Columns on the terrace of the baptistery at Avdat.*
*91. A closer look at the living quarters shown on the left.*

92

93

In the eastern part of the central Negev, that broad arid plain which seems so inhospitable to the unfamiliar eye, the ancient roads that led from Jerusalem and from Gaza to the southern port of Eilat on the Red Sea converge at a spot that the Arabs call Kornub. In ancient times this was the Nabataean city of Mampsis, or Mamshit, a major commercial centre.

The origins of Mampsis-Kornub lie in the Hellenistic era in the Holy Land, when the Hasmonaeans ruled the Kingdom of Judaea and Edom was in decline. The Nabataeans, those mysterious, energetic desert people, had several cities in the southern part of the Holy Land, the best known of which, of course, is the rose-red city of Petra in Transjordan. Their main city in the Negev was Obodah, or Avdat, and they founded Mamshit to serve as a trading city, with a large caravan-serai and warehouses, stables and other public buildings, for the con-

94

95

96

venience of the merchants whose caravans plied the routes of the Middle East. The Romans added a bathhouse and stout ramparts, and later, during the Byzantine era, two churches were built in the city.

Most of what remains of the ancient city dates from the late Nabataean period, characterized by the excellent masonry and distinctive Nabataean capitals. The houses were well fortified, contained several stairwells and had balconies supported by pillars. The Roman city wall enclosed an area of about ten acres. The fortified city thus served to guard the important junction, and for this purpose the ramparts were doubled during Byzantine times.

*92. Nabatean inscription from the southern church of St Theodorus, meaning "U Shu Grandson of An".*
*93. Greek inscription before the altar inside the church.*
*94/97. View of Mamshit.*
*95. Capital from Avdat, depicting a bird.*
*96. Cross from Roman-Byzantine mosaic.*

97

98

In the eastern Negev, where the southern end of the Hebron Hills meets with the Beersheba and Arad valleys, was an Early Bronze Age town. Biblical Arad was situated on the main road to Edom in the east. Here, according to the Bible, dwelt Arad the Canaanite who fought the Children of Israel. "And when Arad the Canaanite, which dwelt in the south, heard tell that Israel came by the way of the spies; then he fought against Israel, and took some of them prisoners" (Num. 21:1). The "way of the spies" refers to the route from Kadesh-Barnea through Atharim.

99

The Israelite defeat occurred at nearby Hormah (Num. 14:45).

Though Canaanite Arad would not yield to the Israelites, who, led by Moses, were sweeping northwest, Joshua was later able to capture the city (Josh. 12:14). The town was then settled by the tribe of Judah and by the Kenites, a people related to the family of Moses.

The Israelites first established a presence here in the 11th century BC, the dawn of the Iron Age. The small, open village from this period found by archaeologists was probably the original Israelite settlement. In the middle of the village there was a raised, crescent-shaped platform with a square altar, possibly the "high place" served by the venerated Kenites. The temple erected on this site in the middle of the 10th century BC is the most important archaeological find. It occupied the northwest corner of the citadel, probably founded by King Solomon. The Arad temple was destroyed and rebuilt six times during the period of the Hebrew monarchies, when the town was an important frontier outpost, until the destruction of the First Temple in Jerusalem in 586 BC. Persian, Hellenistic, Roman and early Arab fortresses were constructed on the same site in the following centuries.

The tell here is also important for the wealth of inscriptions found. Over 200 inscribed potsherds were discovered in the various levels, equally divided between Aramaic and Hebrew. The Aramaic ostraca consist mainly of records of the Persian garrison. The Hebrew inscriptions, on the other hand, date from all periods of the Iron Age and are mostly letters from citadel archives in the surrounding

area. One of these provides the only direct reference to the First Temple that archaeologists have found. In a letter from the archives of one Eliashiv, son of Eshyahu, a mention is made of the "House of Yahweh", doubtlessly a reference to Solomon's Temple.

*98. A typical scene in the arid Negev region.*
*99. Arad was settled in slightly different locations during different historical periods. Here one of the early settlements is seen from the later Tell Arad.*
*100/101. Discoveries made at the tell.*
*102. The restored walls of Tell Arad as seen from afar.*

100

101

102

103

104

Beersheba, the town associated with the Hebrew patriarchs, lies between the prairies of the Negev and the cultivated fields to the north. Hints of its rich history, going back some 6,000 years, are to be found in the nearby ancient tell, eight kilometres east of the modern Israeli town. There, at the bottom level of the tell, archaeologists have discovered oval-shaped caves in the riverbed. These date back to a time when the area was inhabited by semi-nomadic peoples who subsisted mainly on sheep and goat grazing. The caves were entered from above and were covered during dry seasons and rainless years, when the nomads migrated northwards. They were probably the inhabitants of Beersheba when the Hebrew Patriarch, Abraham, made his covenant with Abimelech, Philistine King of Gerar (Gen. 21: 25-33). In return for seven ewe-lambs, the King swore to protect Abraham's well from seizure by

105

his people. In honour of the agreement, the site was named Beersheba, meaning "well of the oath" in Hebrew: "And Abraham planted a grove in Beersheba, and called there on the name of the Lord, the everlasting God" (Gen. 21: 33). The "grove" mentioned in the Bible was probably tamarisk, and the well referred to may, in all likelihood, be like one of those found beside the caves discovered in the archaeological excavations.

Biblical mention of the city of Beersheba is abundant. Abimelech later renewed his covenant there with Isaac, and Jacob, too, it is written, made use of the well: "And Israel took his journey with all that he had, and came to Beersheba, and offered sacrifices unto the God of his father Isaac" (Gen. 46:1). In the Book of Joshua, the site is mentioned as the territory allotted to the tribe of Simeon (19:2). During the time of the Judges, Beersheba was considered the southern frontier of the Israelite territory, as "the congrega tion was gathered together as one man, from Dan even to Beersheba . . ." (Judg. 20:1). This reference, and others like it in the Books of

Samuel, indicate that Beersheba was by then a city of religious and administrative importance.

During the Iron Age, the fortified town of Beersheba was one of four — along with Dan, Beth-El and Gilgal — to be reproached by the Hebrew Prophet Amos, for its rivalry with Jerusalem as the religious centre of Israel. The site is also identified in the Bible as one of the cities whose "high places" were defiled by King Josiah during his religious reforms.

The ancient town of Beersheba was an important caravan stop on the route from Egypt to the Dead Sea, and was probably frequented by Egyptians seeking Dead Sea minerals to be used in embalming. In later periods, the city served as a garrison used by the Maccabees, as well as by Roman and Byzantine soldiers, to protect the southern flank of the cultivated part of the Holy Land.

Modern Beersheba stands atop the former Byzantine site, and several excavations have unearthed houses, tombs, churches and inscriptions dating from this period. Also found were Israelite tombs of the Iron Age. But the most impor-

tant archaeological finds have been made at the tell, where, aside from the ancient network of caves, a royal Israelite fortress has been uncovered.

Many of the articles found at the tell are preserved in the Municipal Museum, originally a 19th-century mosque located inside the city itself, near the "Old Town" founded by the Turks in 1907. Here, too, is the site known as Abraham's Well, although biblical Beersheba is associated with the tell to the east. Also in the originally-Turkish section of town is the colourful Beduin marketplace, an attraction worth visiting on Thursday, the market day. Perhaps more than any other site in the modern town, this *souk* evokes the image of biblical Beersheba, where Abraham — like the Beduin of today — stopped to water his camels.

*103/106. Abraham's Well is located within the modern city of Beersheba. 104/107. The Beduin of Beersheba, who who have been a part of this biblical city for untold years. 105. Sculpture in memory of fallen soldiers. The tell can be faintly distinguished in the distance.*

108

The port city of Ashkelon is first mentioned in the Egyptian "Execration Texts" (two groups of potsherds from the 19th and 20th centuries BC — inscriptions cursing places, and sometimes their rulers, throughout the ancient Middle East). The capture of Ashkelon by Rameses II is depicted in the reliefs at the temple of Karnak in Egypt. There it is shown as a fortified tower. Its conquest by the Philistines — the Sea People, who probably came from Crete — must have taken place in the 12th century BC. In the Book of Judges it is mentioned as one of the Five Cities of the Philistines. It was here that Samson, incensed by the trick played on him by his bride and her compatriots, "slew thirty men of them, and took their spoil, and gave change of garments unto them, which expounded the riddle" (Judg. 14:19).

Later, Ashkelon was one of the many small kingdoms which the Assyrian and Babylonian empires repeatedly overwhelmed. During the Hellenistic period Ashkelon was ruled by the Egyptian-based Ptolemies, as a free port which minted its own coinage. Herod the Great was a native of Ashkelon, and when his power was at its zenith he adorned it with palaces and temples. It remained a Hellenistic city even under Roman rule, its cosmopolitan nature sustained by its flourishing sea and overland trade. Recently a series of splendid sarcophagi, decorated in a lavish Graeco-Roman style, were found near the site of ancient Ashkelon. It seems to have been a workshop where these custom-made stone coffins were produced for wealthy patrons. The most splendid of the sarcophagi may be seen at the Ashkelon National Park, in the modern city.

And did you know that the words "scallion" and "shallot" derive from Ashkelon (Ascalonia, in Latin)? — It must have been famous for its onions, as Falernus was for its wines.

During the Byzantine period Ashkelon had a school of Hellenistic philosophy which was known for its extreme anti-Christian bias. Most of the population was pagan, and worshipped the fish goddess Atargatis, whose upper body was that of a woman, attached to the tail of a fish. The worship of fish deities must have been a very ancient one, dating back to the days of the Philistines, the Sea People, who worshipped Dagon (I Sam. 5:2-5).

This was also a period when Judaism was undergoing a major process of definition and formulation. The Talmud, the great codex of the religious law, was being compiled in the north, in the Galilee and Golan regions. In Ashkelon, too, there were Jews, as attested by the synagogue whose remains were uncovered in modern times. The Jewish community survived the many rules, the rise and fall of empires that dominated the Middle East. The Abbasid dynasty, whose seat was in Mesopotamia,

109

succeeded the Byzantines from Asia Minor. When the Crusaders took Jerusalem and all but destroyed its Jewish community, the Jews of Ashkelon gave shelter to the survivors. This congregation also ransomed captives and purchased ritual objects which had been looted by the European conquerors from the synagogues of Jerusalem. Then the Christian knights conquered Ashkelon itself, but by this time their zeal had somewhat abated, and the Jews were allowed to go on living in the city as before. After the Moslem reconquest in 1187, the city's ramparts were destroyed, and its population dispersed. The Moslem quarter of Ashkelon was rebuilt, but was again destroyed in the late 13th century. The city never recovered its ancient and medieval glory. During the 400 years of Ottoman rule it went into a decline, and its population was negligible. The small port continued to function, and shipping agents would stay in the area to conduct

their business. The sands drifted and covered the last vestiges of the historic city of Ashkelon.

In the 19th century an Englishwoman, Lady Hester Stanhope, persuaded the Turkish pasha in Acre that there was buried treasure in the tell of Ashkelon, beside the sea. Consequently, hundreds of Arab workmen were sent to dig it up. They found no treasure, but hundreds of splendid archaeological finds were uncovered, from various periods, chiefly Roman and Byzantine. Unfortunately, many of the pieces were removed and incorporated in buildings in Jaffa and Acre.

*108. Roman-style statue of Egyptian goddess Isis with Horus.*
*109. The Roman forum, located in the national park of Ashkelon.*
*110. Nike, the winged goddess of victory, stands atop the world, borne on the shoulders of Atlas.*
*111. A Roman stone sarcophagus in Ashkelon, placed near the Roman forum. This was one of a number of sarcophagi found in this area — probably in a local workshop for custom-made coffins.*

112

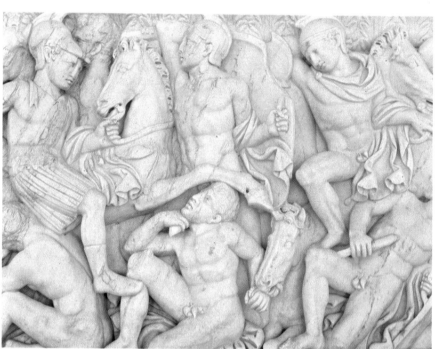

113

114

The modern city of Ashkelon is situated some 3.5 kilometres northeast of the tell. Originally founded as the city of Majdal by the Egyptian governor in 1830, it was a small town that subsisted chiefly by fishing, until the middle of the 20th century, when it began to grow. After the establishment of the State of Israel, a Jewish town by the name of Migdal-Ashkelon began to grow beside the fishing town of Majdal. Surrounded by rolling sand-dunes and orchards, it is a popular seaside resort. The tell area has been incorporated in a national park beside the city, and here, amid soft lawns and pleasant woods, are dotted statues, columns and capitals from the Graeco-Roman and Byzantine periods. The combination of Mediterranean beaches, parks and archaeological excavations is particularly appealing.

112. Detail of a Roman stone sarcophagus, depicting two lovers.
113. The handsomest of the sarcophagi discovered at Ashkelon, this detailed carving, in high relief, depicts Roman soldiers in fierce battle with barbarians.
114. Remains of the ramparts built at Ashkelon by the Crusaders.
115. Ever since biblical times the coast of Philistia was renowned for its fertile lands. Nowadays the Ashkelon region is famous for its rich orange groves.
116. The ruins of a Byzantine church stand above a field of spring flowers near Beth-Shemesh.

115

116

117

118

Two kilometres separate Beth-Guvrin and Mareshah in the Judaean foothills south of Jerusalem. These ancient cities have been integrally linked by archaeological finds and historical events. Mareshah is identified in the Book of Joshua (15:44) as a city of the tribe of Judah; it was later fortified by King Rehoboam and served to protect Jerusalem (II Chr. 11:8). Until the Parthian conquest of 40 BC, Mareshah served as the capital city of the Edomites. Its prominent place was then usurped by the neighbouring Beth-Guvrin, which continued to serve as a district capital (under the name of Eleutheropolis) in Roman times. Not even the Mameluke conquest of 1244 reduced the city's importance.

Evidence of the ancient greatness of Mareshah and Beth-Guvrin is found in their ruins. In the latter city, the remains of a 3rd-century synagogue were uncovered, as were the mosaic floors of a 5th- or 6th-century church, and the Crusader Church of St Anna. Mareshah, on the other hand, is famous mainly for its 63 limestone caves. These bell-shaped cavities, hollowed out by ancient seafaring Phoenicians — who used the soft inside of the rock to build their magnificent port of Ashkelon — served as tombs, living quarters and for pressing grapes and olives. The caves are quite impressive in size, the largest measuring 22 metres in length and 17.4 metres in width. Their sloping walls, together with the play of light entering through apertures in the ceilings, create the illusion of even greater dimensions.

The sheer profusion and unsurpassed richness of the carved ornamentation at Mareshah, made possible by the softness of the limestone, immediately strikes the eye as one enters the caves. One descends the rock-hewn steps, holding on to the banisters, which are unique to the site. Along the walls, numerous carved-out niches and pillars can be seen. The drawings covering the burial chambers display a mixture of Egyptian and Greek styles — a rare combination. Similar cave drawings have been discovered in Ptolemaic tombs in Alexandria and in Phoenician burial chambers dating from the Hellenistic period.

In the largest cave, whose architectural and ornamental design is the most complex, one passes through a large entrance hall (an altar apparently once stood on the left), an ornamented portal and a hallway leading to three burial chambers. The paramount role of the Hellenistic ornamentation quickly becomes apparent. A recess in the middle of one burial chamber is decorated with a pediment bearing a stylized leaf design of the kind found in Greek temples. On either side of the triangular form stand eagles with outstretched wings perched upon yellow tables, each of which is supported by three lions' feet. Below the pediment runs a Doric frieze depicting animals and hunting scenes. Elaborate wreaths decorate the entire length of the wall.

Focusing on the portal, one notices two red pilasters, with rosettes beneath their capitals. On either side are tall, black amphorae with red or white bands, long wreaths streaming from their mouths. Near the entrance to the hallway is a depiction of Cerberus, the three-headed, dragon-tailed dog who guards the gateway to the Underworld in Greek mythology, permitting all to enter but none to depart.

Chiselled in the walls of the cave are many inscriptions in Greek dating from 196 to 119 BC. One presents a poetic dialogue between two lovers (variously interpreted as a poem or a letter); another mentions the priest Miron and the woman Kalypso. Markings can also be discerned from Byzantine times, when crosses and altars were often etched in the soft rock by monks who inhabited the caves. The adjacent tell of Sandahanna gets its name from these hermits, who called the mound after St John (John is Hanna in Arabic).

Inscriptions in this, the largest and most elaborate of the caves, indicate that it belonged to the family of one Apollophanes, son of Sesmios, the head of the Sidonian colony in Mareshah for 33 years. Significantly, the names of the older generation of the family were Hebraic, whereas later generations bore Greek names, indicating a gradual process of Hellenization.

The basic design of the largest cave is repeated, although on a smaller scale, in most of the other hollowed-out rocks. Elaborate garlands, amphorae and wreaths, entire scenes, and carved ornaments, such as pilasters and friezes, adorn many of the burial chambers; inscriptions and other carvings by unknown hands are likewise great in number.

*117. Cross carved by pilgrims.*
*118. A group of visitors in the interior of one of the caves.*
*119. Example of the cave openings, responsible for the unique lighting effects.*

120

Apart from the decorations of the caves themselves, a number of archaeological finds have been turned up at Mareshah. For example, excavations begun in 1900 unearthed a figure of Aphrodite, bone and glass fragments and cosmetics, all dating from the 3rd and 4th centuries AD. Incidentally, the discovery of some of the tombs was unwittingly aided by grave robbers in search of treasure on the site.

A more recent archaeological undertaking in 1972 has revealed the existence of a new cave, nine metres long and four metres high.

No less than 200 niches are hewn out of its walls, some containing pottery from the Hellenistic period, both locally-produced and imported. Four lamps were found in one niche, and other pieces of pottery, some in perfect or near-perfect condition, were discovered lying along the walls. Also unearthed were the bones of goats, pigs and sheep.

So much of the world of antiquity has been preserved in these caves, be it the fleeting emotions of lovers touchingly recorded for posterity, or the purposeful and painstaking adornment of burial grounds. A

121

visit to the area of Beth-Guvrin and Mareshah provides the curious and the observant with a wealth of information about human lives lived many hundreds of years ago.

*120. Entrance to the underground tomb of the Sidonian colony.*
*121. Hole in top of cave — later used for letting down prisoners.*
*122. In spring the entire landscape comes to life with flowers, as it did thousands of years ago when the nearby tombs were first carved out of the underground rock.*
*123. One of the tombs at Mareshah — its size and elaborate design suggest that it belonged to a prominent family. The ornamentation clearly bears the influence of Hellenistic style. Note the use of pediments and columns.*

122

123

In the course of the millennia, how many people have made their way up to the city of Jerusalem? No one can tell, but it must be millions. Some of the routes have not changed, only their surface evolved, so to speak, from dirt path to paved road to the modern tarmac. One ancient road that is well preserved is the Roman way to Jerusalem that runs through the Elah Valley, connecting Jerusalem with Beth-Guvrin and Gaza.

During the long period of Roman rule in the Holy Land this was a much used route. Both Josephus and Pliny described it and the villages that lay along the way. Much of it is in the form of broad steps, far apart and each quite low, so that a horse could manage them easily. All along it they set up milestones, both to commemorate the construction of the road, and give due thanks to the reigning ruler and to mark the distance from the city of Jerusalem, or Aelia Capitolina, as the Romans renamed it after the second Jewish revolt.

These milestones were an effective reminder to the travellers of the mighty power that ruled over the land and its inhabitants. Many milestones were found along the Beth-Guvrin route, and these have been set up beside the road, where they can be seen and read by the modern traveller. They are between 150 and 250 centimetres in height, and of identical form — a square base, on which rests a cylindrical stone bearing the inscription.

*124. Roman structure near Beth-Shemesh, on the road to Jerusalem.*
*125. Roman milestone on the Beth-Guvrin road.*
*126. Group of Roman milestones on the road from Jerusalem to Beth-Guvrin.*
*127. The rock-hewn Roman road which ran through the Elah Valley, connecting Jerusalem with Beth-Guvrin and Gaza.*

124

125

126

127

128

129

One of the oldest, continuously inhabited cities in the world, Hebron is also one of the most beautiful. Surrounded by vineyards and olive groves, it is almost as rich in biblical associations as Jerusalem. The Bible tells us that Hebron, inhabited by the "children of Anak" — the giants — was built seven years before Zoan in Egypt. This would pin down the establishment of Hebron to about 1730 BC, but archaeological excavations have shown that agricultural communities lived there as far back as the Chalcolithic and Early Bronze Age, i.e., about 1,500 years earlier.

The Book of Genesis (Chapter 23) tells us how Abraham bought the Cave of the Machpelah, which was at the end of the field belonging to Ephron the Hittite, to serve as a burial place for Sarah. "And Abraham weighed to Ephron the silver, which he had named in the audience of the sons of Heth, four hundred shekels of silver, current money with the merchant. And the field of Ephron, which was in Machpelah, which was before Mamre, the field, and the cave which was therein, and all the trees that were in the field, that were in all the borders around it, were made sure." This innocent transaction, meticulously recorded, was to place Hebron firmly in the centre of historical events.

130

131

132                          133                                                        134

Between the time of Abraham and that of Moses, while the Children of Israel were in Egypt's "house of bondage", Hebron was inhabited by Hittites from northern Syria, who administered the area on behalf of the Hyksos, the "Shepherd Kings" ruling Egypt at this time. The town flourished, and the fame of its vineyards spread far and wide. When Moses sent men into the land of Canaan, to see "what the land is, whether it be fat or lean", they reached the brook of Eshcol near Hebron, and there cut off a branch with a single cluster of grapes, which was so heavy that "they bore it with two men upon a staff"! Later, when the tribes settled in Canaan, Hebron came within the portion of Judah, and it was there that David reigned for seven years, before making Jerusalem his capital.

Hebron was a centre of religious pilgrimage from the Israelite period on. For, after Sarah, Abraham,

Isaac and his wife Rebecca, Jacob and Leah were also buried in the Cave of the Machpelah. (According to Moslem tradition, Noah was also buried there.)

Later the Edomites, a Judaized tribe from the Transjordanian desert, settled in the town. The place was partly destroyed by the Romans when they crushed the great Jewish revolt (AD 70). However, it remained inhabited, and during the Byzantine period churches and synagogues were built there. Since the Arabs conquered the Holy Land, Hebron has been an Islamic centre.

At the heart of Hebron is the famous "Haram al Khaleel" — the Shrine of the Friend — which marks the site of the Machpelah. It is a massive building that dominates its surroundings. The base of the present edifice dates back to the reign of Herod the Great, who built the shrine, as he did the Temple in Jerusalem, of great

square-cut stones called ashlars. A mosque was added in the 7th century, and was converted by the Crusaders into a church, only to revert to its original character after the Mamelukes conquered the country. It was the Mameluke Baibars who developed Hebron, and built the massive structure we see today. It was he who decreed that Jews, who had worshipped at this shrine since the time of Abraham, might not go further than the first five steps into the cave. This rule came to an end in 1967, and today Jews and Moslems both worship in the place where their forefather Abraham is buried.

*128. Staircase leading to the Cave of Machpelah.*
*129. Herodian wall of the Machpelah.*
*130. View of the Machpelah edifice with the minaret tower on the left.*
*131. Glass blowing is a traditional craft in Hebron.*
*132. Interior of mosque in the Machpelah.*
*133. Decorative grille in the Machpelah.*
*134. Tomb of the Patriarch Abraham.*

135

136

"And it came to pass in the days when the judges ruled, that there was famine in the land. And a certain man of Bethlehem-Judah went to sojourn in the country of Moab, and his wife, and his two sons." Thus begins the Book of Ruth, which tells the story of the two widows, the old and the young, the returning native and the stranger, who came to glean in the fields of Boaz the Bethlehemite "in the beginning of the barley harvest".

The wonderful pastoral scenes that emerge in the course of the story are easily visualized in the landscape of Bethlehem to this day. Against the backdrop of the Judaean mountains, almost ethereal in their violet starkness against the sky, the softened contours of the terraced hills of Bethlehem present a serene setting for one of the holiest places in the world.

It was in Bethlehem that David was born, Jesse's youngest son, whom the Prophet Samuel, disappointed in King Saul, took from amongst the sheep and anointed as the future king of Israel. David was a descendant of Ruth and Boaz — and Mary, the mother of Jesus, was a descendant of the House of David. Thus the lineage is preserved and the place imbued with eternal Messianic associations.

Unlike Jerusalem, Bethlehem was never a grand capital, and it has retained its engagingly modest rural simplicity. In the 4th century, Helena, the mother of Constantine the Great, marked the site of the birth of Jesus by building a Byzantine basilica there. But this original Church of the Nativity did not last very long. In the 6th century, in the reign of Justinian, it was destroyed and another built in its place. This church escaped the destruction that the Persian invaders wreaked on most of the Christian property in the Holy Land. Legend has it that the reason it was spared was that the mosaic on

137

the western façade of the church depicted, amongst other things, the rulers of the Persian Empire — which so impressed the conquerors that they left the building intact. When the Arabs invaded the country they too respected the church and did not damage it.

It was in this church, on Christmas Day in the year 1100, that the Frankish Crusader Baldwin was crowned king. The church saw other conquerors come and go, and remained more or less untouched, but under Ottoman rule friction between the several Christian communities over possession of the Church of the Nativity became very heated. The mysterious disappearance of the silver star marking the birthplace of Jesus in the crypt beneath the church intensified the rancour and mutual accusations between the Eastern and Western

Christians, and was one of the pretexts for the outbreak of the Crimean War. After this war, which ended in 1856, the Turkish sultan issued a *firman* (royal decree) guaranteeing the *status quo* in the various holy places and their sanctuaries. This has served to freeze the situation more or less until the present, but has not prevented many small disputes from arising

in the relations between the various churches and sects.

Since the 19th century, pilgrimage to the Holy Land has increased constantly, and Bethlehem has become the focus of annual Christmas celebrations which grow ever bigger. On Christmas Eve, at midnight, a colourful procession leaves the Catholic church adjoining that of the Nativity and enters the

*135-137. Sheep tended by Arab shepherd in the fields of Bethlehem — a scene largely unchanged since biblical times.*
*138. Interior of the Church of the Nativity in Bethlehem.*
*139. The entrance to the grotto of the Nativity.*
*140. General view of Bethlehem.*

crypt. Bells ring out from the many belfries all over the town. The surrounding streets are filled to burst-

*141. Residents and visitors stroll through the streets of modern-day Bethlehem, carrying on their everyday affairs.*
*142. Place of the Manger in the grotto.*
*143. An altar in the Church of the Nativity. Above it hangs a painting depicting Jesus and his Apostles at the Last Supper.*
*144. A silver star marks the place of the Nativity.*

141

ing with pilgrims, and the procession is televised and broadcast live to viewers all over the world.

Bethlehem's churches reflect the great variety of the Christian world. There are Roman Catholic, Greek Othodox and Armenian churches here, vying with each other in their proximity to the holy place and in the magnificence of their appointments. As well as the sacred crypt, you may also see under the Church of the Nativity the cell wherein St Jerome lived, in the 4th century, when he was translating the Bible from Hebrew into Latin. He was among the many monks who flocked to the Holy Land in that period and settled in small hermitages around the holy places. Here in this cell, it is said, St Jerome lived for many years, and even the wild beasts kept him company and never harmed him while he was at his sacred labour. Two noble Roman ladies, Paula and her daughter Eustochium, who had accompanied Jerome to Bethlehem, had a monastery built near the Church of the Nativity, probably on the site now occupied by the Franciscan monastery.

142

143

144

Returning to his native land after decades of voluntary exile in Padan Aram, Jacob the Patriarch was accompanied by a multitude of wives, concubines, sons, man-servants, maid-servants, great herds of cattle and camels. "And they journeyed from Beth-El and there was but a little way to come to Eph-rath, and Rachel travailed and she had a hard labour. And it came to pass, when she was in hard labour, that the midwife said to her, 'Fear not, thou shalt have this son also'. And it came to pass, as her soul was departing (for she died) that she called his name Ben-Oni, but his father called him Benjamin. And Rachel died, and was buried on the way to Ephrath, which is Bethlehem. And Jacob set a pillar over her grave, that is the pillar of Rachel's grave unto this day" (Gen. 35:16-20).

Thus, Rachel is the only one of the matriarchs who is not buried in the Cave of the Machpelah in Hebron.

Rachel's tomb on the road between Bethlehem and Jerusalem is mentioned in ancient sources. According to descriptions of Jewish travellers in the Middle Ages, the monument consisted of 11 stones, laid by the 11 sons of Jacob, top-ped by a large stone, laid by Jacob himself. The tomb was later roofed by a dome supported by four pil-lars, and at the end of the 18th century was enclosed by walls. At the end of the 19th century the great Anglo-Jewish philanthropist, Sir Moses Montefiore, found the tomb in a ruined state when he visited it, and had it restored. The tomb is a traditional focus of pil-grimage for Jewish women who wish to have a child or fear a difficult birth.

*145. As Rachel, the much-loved wife of Jacob, was childless for most of her years and died bearing his youngest son, it became customary among Jewish women to pray at her tomb, hoping to cure bar-renness or avoid a difficult birth.*
*146. The many prayerbooks to the right testify to the large numbers who come to Rachel's Tomb. Here two women pray in front of the embroidered velvet cloth which covers the Holy Ark.*
*147. View of the dome-topped tomb as seen from the road leading to Jerusalem.*

145

146

147

148

148/150. Mosaic synagogue floor in
Susiya, with Hebrew inscription.
149. Columns once flanking the entrance
of Susiya synagogue.
151. Partially damaged mosaic on Susiya

synagogue floor depicting the menorah
and Holy Ark.
152. Decorative design with inscription.
153. The synagogue at Susiya after
restoration.

At one time it was believed that
Jewish presence in the Holy Land
in Byzantine times was limited to
the Galilee and Golan regions. But
this long-standing fallacy has now
been corrected by the discovery of
two late 4th-century synagogues
in Eshtemoa and Susiya (mentioned in Joshua, 21:14 and 19:5),
towns lying a few kilometres apart
on the edge of the Judaean desert,
south of Hebron. The archaeological finds in these sites suggest that

149

150

151

152

a Jewish community flourished in the area south of Jerusalem until after the Arab conquest in the 7th century. In fact, the synagogue at Susiya may not have been destroyed until the arrival of the Crusaders.

The remains at Eshtemoa stand at the highest point of the modern-day Arab village of Samoa. The synagogue's damaged mosaic floor is flanked by four pillars. Five earthenware jars from the Israelite era were discovered on the site by an Arab foreman. At Susiya, there are a pair of candelabra (*menorahs*) flanking the Holy Ark depicted on the mosaic floor. Other religious symbols are also shown, such as the

153

154

155

ram's horn and the palm frond. The Hebrew inscription is one of the few dating from the early Byzantine period.

As well as being mentioned in the Book of Joshua, Eshtemoa is also named as one of the places to which King David sent presents after the defeat of the Amalekites (I Sam. 30:28). In the Roman and Byzantine periods, Eshtemoa was a substantial Jewish town, which was mentioned in some sources as Astemo. The synagogue dating from that period was discovered in 1935, in archaeological excavations near the mosque in the present-day village.

The synagogue measures 13 by 21 metres, and is impressive for its fine masonry. Entrance was gained by three doors in the long eastern wall. The Holy Ark, where the scroll of the Torah was kept, was in a large niche in the northern wall

(Jerusalem is north of Eshtemoa), flanked by two smaller niches. These may have contained candelabra.

In 1970 the site was cleared and some of the structure restored, and in the process a large hoard of Iron Age silver jewellery and ingots was discovered. As this was found beneath the synagogue floor, it suggests that an Israelite silver-smith must have had a workshop on this site some time before the synagogue was built, probably in the early days of the kingdom. It has also been proposed that the hoard may have been part of the booty that King David sent the elders of Eshtemoa after his victory over the Amalekites.

The synagogue is remarkably well preserved, with a portion of the western wall rising to a height of 8.5 metres. The roof rested on columns set in square bases. The

parts of the mosaic floor that remain are decorated with floral and geometric designs, as well as various traditional symbols. A large Aramaic inscription in the southern section of the floor names a certain Lazar the Priest and his sons as the donors of money for the construction of the synagogue.

The Eshtemoa synagogue is of a distinctive form, quite unusual among the ancient synagogues in the Holy Land. Its size and the quality of its construction testify to the prosperity of the community that built it, in this era, and that seems to have been assimilated by the subsequent Moslem population.

156

157

About five kilometres south of Bethlehem, in a pleasant hollow surrounded by orchards and vineyards, there are three large rectangular water pools, partially carved out of the living rock and partially constructed. They are known as Solomon's Pools, because tradition ascribes them to the reign of that wise monarch. In reality the pools were built during the Second Temple period, probably in the reign of Herod the Great. The pools are between 120 and 170 metres long, about 70 metres wide and between 7 and 15 metres deep. Their combined volume is about 160,000 cubic metres, which was a very large amount in the days when they were built, and was probably meant to supply both the Herodion fortress to the south and Jerusalem to the north.

The ground here is higher than the city of Jerusalem, and the rain and underground spring water that collects in these pools is easily led to the city by force of gravity. Remains of the conduits along which the water was carried are to be seen in various places on the way to Jerusalem.

In the 19th century, attracted by the abundance of water — a rare enough commodity in the country as a whole — missionaries attempted to settle in the vicinity of the pools. Though the settlement failed, one of its enterprises remained, namely, the introduction of honey bees into the agriculture of the region. The square fort near the pools was built in the 17th century.

*154/155. Byzantine architraves above entrance to Eshtemoa synagogue.*
*156/157. Mosaic patterns and carved stone ornament the synagogue.*
*158. Approach to Solomon's pools.*
*159/160. Two of the three pools.*

158

159

160

In the 5th century, when Christianity was spreading rapidly throughout the Middle East and southern Europe, many hermits came to the Holy Land and devoted themselves to contemplation in remote valleys and in the nooks and crannies of the Judaean desert, with its rich biblical associations.

Born in Cappadocia in the year AD 439, the monk Saba went first to Jerusalem and then spent several years in monasteries all over the country. After living alone for five years in a cave in the Valley of Kidron, he had a vision which led him to the place where he built his church. There are many miraculous tales about Mar (Saint) Saba, who lived to be 93 years old. He founded many monasteries in Judaea, as well as several hostels for pilgrims in Jerusalem and Jericho. In his lifetime there were 150 monks in his own monastery and 120 in the one he founded at Tekoah.

In the course of the centuries the fortunes of the monastery rose and fell. In 614 it was attacked by the invading Persians, and in the 8th and 9th centuries by marauding nomads. Fortifications were added for the protection of the monks, and during the Crusaders' kingdom it flourished. Later it was almost destroyed, but was never abandoned. In the 19th century Imperial Russia undertook to rebuild the monastery and protect it. It was constructed as a fortress on four levels, and the western keep was made so stout as to withstand a heavy attack or siege. There are 110 rooms in the present monastery.

Today there are only seven monks living in Mar Saba. It may be visited — by men only — at noontime. The principal chapel

161

162

163

houses the remains of the saint. In the courtyard is the tomb of John of Damascus, the historian of the Byzantine Church, who lived and worked here in the 8th century. Other famous monks lived in the monastery, such as St Cyril of Beth-Shean, who, in the 6th century, wrote the history of Othymius, Saba's spiritual father, and his famous disciple.

The original church, dating back to the saint's lifetime, is in a cavern west of the courtyard. It is ornately decorated, some of the murals going back to Byzantine times. In one of the cavern walls there is a deep recess, containing hundreds of skulls — the remains of monks who were killed in the many attacks and invasions the monastery has known in its long history.

On one of the narrow terraces the monks have cultivated a small garden. There are two palm trees, reputed to be slips of the date palm which sustained Mar Saba in his solitude, a few olive trees, a fig tree and some pines. They are watered by the sparse stream of the spring which Mar Saba had discovered in a vision.

The monastery's library contains one of the world's oldest manuscripts of the Septuagint, the ancient Greek translation of the Bible.

164

165

166

167

161. Kidron Valley, as seen from the Mar Saba monastery on the hilltop.
162. Part of the monastery, with fortress wall behind it.
163. Campanile of the Mar Saba monastery, overlooking the Kidron Valley.
164/165. Father Iosiph of the Greek Orthodox monastery of Mar Saba opens the gate with an outsize key.
166. The St Nicholas chapel. Note skulls of monks inside cupboards.
167. The embalmed body of St Saba.
168. (overleaf) The inner court of Mar Saba.

On a hill southeast of Bethlehem stands the desert retreat and mausoleum of Herod the Great. About 50 years after the Judaean ruler's death, Herodion was occupied by Jewish rebels holding out against the Romans and, during the Byzantine period, the site was inhabited by Christian hermits.

The castle of Herodion was one of King Herod's finest architectural endeavours. Josephus, describing the site as "an artificial rounded hill in the form of a breast", gave a meticulous description of the extensive work of construction: "The crest Herod crowned with a ring of round towers, the enclosure was filled with gorgeous palaces, the magnificent appearance of which was not confined to the interior of the apartments, but outer walls, battlements and roofs all had wealth lavished upon them . . .". Some indication of its elaborate design is shown by the

*169. View of Herodion.*
*170. Herodion as seen from a distance, between the church spire and the mosque dome.*

169

170

168

171

172

173

Corinthian and Nabataean capitals found on the remains of many of the courtyard columns. Stucco was frequently employed for the finer details on the pillars, providing intricate patterns not unlike those found at nearby Masada. Also discovered among the ruins was a large Roman bath with a mosaic floor.

Herod first made use of this desert retreat during a power struggle in Jerusalem, when he and his family took refuge at the site. Later, at the height of his power, he had double circular retaining walls added, and transformed the mound into a mausoleum and fortress; obsessed with fear of enemies, he considered the fortifications as his only means of escaping, after his death, the desecration of his body by the populace of Judaea. Thus, Herodion was to serve both as an ornate tomb and a protective fortress.

The elaborate details of Herod's funeral, remarkable for its splendour, even in this period of the Roman Empire, are provided by Josephus: "The bier was of solid gold, studded with precious stones, and had a covering of purple, embroidered with various colours: on this lay the body enveloped in a purple robe, a diadem encircling the head . . . The body was thus conveyed to Herodion, where, in accordance with the directions of the deceased, it was interred". But one question remains unanswered: where within the confines of the castle was Herod buried?

During the early centuries of the Christian era, the ruins of Herodion were occupied by Christian hermits, as shown by numerous inscriptions, coins and other marks of habitation.

83

Chesalon is mentioned in the Book of Joshua 15:10 as a border town in the territory of Judah. It was also known as Har Jearim, which means, the wooded mountain. The town of Chesalon still existed in the days of Eusebius, the 4th-century Church Father, whose descriptions of the Holy Land are of tremendous value to its historians. Archaeological investigation of the local tell showed that it was inhabited continuously from the Israelite period through the Second Temple and Roman era, and as late as the early Arab period in the Holy Land. Thereafter it was abandoned until modern times.

In 1951 a modern agricultural village, organized on a cooperative basis, was founded in Chesalon. Its population, which numbers some 240, cultivates fruit orchards and poultry.

In 1969 Israeli sculptor Nathan Rapaport chose Chesalon as the location for a huge monument which he called "Scrolls of Fire", dedicated to the history of the Jewish people. Rising some 7.5 metres, the cast metal monument is covered with bold relief figures symbolizing the millennial history of the people whose ancient home this was, and who were persecuted in many countries and through many centuries, before returning to their ancient homeland. One part of the relief is a visual paraphrase of the triumphal arch of Titus in Rome — where the latter depicts the

treasures of the Temple being carried away by the victorious Roman soldiers, Rapaport shows the great candelabrum being brought back by young Jewish men in modern dress.

Not far from a road leading up to Jerusalem, the monument is a part of the landscape and its history, because in a way it expresses its soul.

Other monuments by Rapaport are world famous — one stands at the site of the Warsaw Ghetto, having been commissioned by the Polish government after the war; another, also dedicated to the heroes of that ghetto's uprising, is at the Israeli kibbutz of Yad Mordechai.

174

175

*171. Ballistic stones at Herodion.*
*172. Interior of Herodion fortress.*
*173. Judaean Desert seen from Herodion.*
*174/175. Details of "Scrolls of Fire".*
*176. General view of the monument.*

176

The tranquil village of Ein Karem (Arabic, the Spring of the Vineyard), in northern Jerusalem, clings to the Judaean hillside, its low-lying houses dwarfed by the tapering cypresses which rise from the slopes. Some scholars believe the present-day village to correspond to the biblical Bet Hakerem. Ein Karem is sacred to Christianity as the traditional birthplace of John the Baptist. Here stands the Church of the Visitation, commanding a breathtaking view of the valley below.

This church and its monastery, which belong to the Franciscan Order, mark the place where the house of John the Baptist and his family is believed to have stood. Inside there is a sacred relic — a stone into which, tradition says, the saint disappeared when the Roman soldiers came for him.

Within the church there are remains of a two-storied Crusader church, which had fallen into disuse after the fall of the Christian kingdom in the Holy Land. In 1679 the Franciscan Order purchased the ruin and restored it in part.

*177. St. Mary's Well at Ein Karem.*
*178. General View of Ein Karem.*
*179. View of the Old City of Jerusalem with Mount Scopus and Temple Mount in the background.*

177

178

180

The Second Temple, when first built by the exiles after their return from Babylon, was a modest affair compared to Solomon's Temple. Later, Herod the Great made it his most ambitious building project, enlarging the temple itself, adding palaces and citadels beside and around it, developing the environs of the Upper City, until it became known among contemporaries as one of the handsomest building complexes in the world.

In the year AD 70 Jerusalem was almost totally destroyed when the Roman legions succeeded in crushing the first great Jewish revolt. The Temple was devastated and never rebuilt. The only part that remained standing was a portion of the retaining wall on the western side of the Temple Mount, and it has survived to this day. Known as the Western or "Wailing" Wall, it is the site most precious to the Jews since the dispersion.

In recent years archaeological excavations have revealed many additional parts of the Temple Mount complex that had been hidden under the surface — south of the Mount a majestic staircase, that led to the Double ("Hulda") Gates,

181

182

183

which can still be seen; on the western side, remains of arches and staircases that led from the Lower City to the Upper; a stone on which were carved the words, "To the Place of Trumpeting", in Hebrew, and several other fascinating remains.

The sanctity of Jerusalem has always attracted the more orthodox Jews, and, to this day, there are several quarters in the city where a strictly traditional way of life is maintained. In these neighbourhoods, children attend special religious infant and primary schools, in which they are educated in the traditional manner, with hardly any modern subjects in the curriculum. Men and women dress in the old way, the men in black frock-coats and hats, invariably bearded and with the traditional sidelocks.

*180. Men's section of the Western Wall in the northern half of the plaza.*
*181/182. Worshippers pray at the Wall.*
*183. Notes bearing prayers.*
*184. Second Temple model at the Holy Land Hotel.*
*185. Signs requesting modest dress of visitors to orthodox Mea Shearim.*
*186-188. Synagogues in the Old City of Jerusalem.*

189

190

191

Stone, the substance of Jerusalem and its only resource, is worked in a variety of techniques — it is left rough, semi-smooth or polished like satin; it is carved in many elaborate styles; its subtle tones, from warm rose through cream to dazzling white, are matched and contrasted.

A characteristic feature of Jerusalem architecture, that recurs through the many styles and periods, are the twin windows — they are topped with Gothic, Romanesque or Moorish arches, embellished with pillars or scrolls, demurely shuttered with rustic wooden blinds or richly filled with stained glass.

The Rockefeller Museum of Antiquities, built in the 1930s with the help of the Rockefeller family, was the country's principal museum during the British Mandate. It is inspired by the style of the Crusader fortresses, a style that the architects of the British Government favoured throughout their building projects in the Holy Land. It is particularly appropriate on this site, for the museum stands on the hill from which, in July 1099, the Frankish princes and knights launched their attack on Saracen Jerusalem.

A totally different style was employed in building *Yad Vashem*, the memorial to the victims of the Holocaust, symbolizing the determination of the Jewish people never to forget, as well as their hope for a better future. The name *Yad Vashem* is taken from a verse in the Book of Isaiah: "Even unto them will I give in mine house and within my walls *a place and a name* . . ." (56:5). The memorial is built in the simplest, barest style, rough-hewn stone with bands of reinforced concrete, without any ornamentation.

One of the most striking landmarks in modern Jerusalem is the Shrine of the Book, which is a part of the Israel Museum complex. The white dome of the shrine and the square black slab behind it represent "The War of the Sons of Light with the Sons of Darkness", the theme of one of the Dead Sea Scrolls. The interior of the shrine is designed to look like a natural cave, with a tunnel leading to the round room above which is suspended the white dome. Along the tunnel and under the dome are displayed the scrolls which were discovered near the Dead Sea and in the Judaean desert between 1947 and the 1960s. Also on display are some artifacts found together with the scrolls.

Yet another modern monument of architectural interest is the John F. Kennedy Memorial. Built in the form of a felled tree, each of the curved concrete and glass strips, of which the structure is composed, bears the seal of one of the states of the United States of America.

192

193

*189. The house of Beit Thabor, located in an old Jewish neighbourhood, was built in the 19th century by the architect and explorer, Conrad Schick.*
*190. The Laemel School, named after the Austrian Jewish philanthropist, Simon von Laemel.*
*191. Crusader architectural style was employed in the design of the Rockefeller Museum of Antiquities, built in the 1930s by the British.*
*192. The decorative wall and gate which mark the entrance to* Yad Vashem, *the memorial to the victims of the Holocaust.*
*193. The white-domed Shrine of the Book at the Israel Museum displays the famous Dead Sea Scrolls.*
*194. The unusual architectural design of the John F. Kennedy Memorial captures the eye.*

194

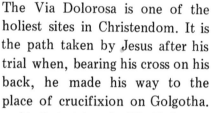

The Via Dolorosa is one of the holiest sites in Christendom. It is the path taken by Jesus after his trial when, bearing his cross on his back, he made his way to the place of crucifixion on Golgotha.

At first sight, the Via Dolorosa seems like any other street in the Old City, with its picturesque archways and the interplay of light and shade. A closer look reveals the churches that mark the nine Stations of the Cross along the way. The shrines bear the number of the Station they represent, each one commemorating one of the dramatic incidents which took place on Jesus' last journey.

The last five Stations on the Via Dolorosa are located inside the Church of the Holy Sepulchre, which stands on a rise called Golgotha, an Aramaic word meaning skull. Christian tradition has it that the place was so named because the skull of the first man was found there. The original structure was built in Byzantine times, but it was the Crusaders who gave it the architectural style we see today.

91

JERUSALEM THE ETERNAL

200

201

202

The rights and possessions of each of the Christian sects that share the Church of the Holy Sepulchre — Greek Orthodox, Roman Catholic, Armenian, Coptic and Syrian — were defined in 1852, in a document known as the *Status Quo*, which is still in force. The current restoration of the Church began in 1955, and is still going on. The Armenian chapel built above the Sepulchre itself is one of the recent additions.

The churches of the Old City of Jerusalem attract pilgrims from all over the world, all year round, but during the festivals, and especially at Christmas and Easter, there are thousands of visitors thronging the churches. The rites of the various sects are celebrated in all their traditional splendour, and chanting is heard in Greek, Armenian and Latin. The brocaded robes and magnificent altar cloths of the Eastern churches lend a particular glow to the atmosphere of worship. The brilliant colours of the chapels, the light that pours in through the stained-glass windows, evoke the grandeur of medieval religious spectacles.

*195. Street sign on the Via Dolorosa.*
*196/197. The traditional procession of Christian pilgrims along the Via Dolorosa on Friday afternoon.*
*198/199. General view and façade of the Church of the Holy Sepulchre.*
*200. Armenian bishop reading the Gospel at the tomb of Christ.*
*201. Greek bishop celebrating Mass at the tomb of Christ.*
*202. Service in the Armenian church on the feast day of St. James.*
*203. Armenian priest reading prayers to young people before Holy Communion.*
*204. St. John's Chapel at the Russian nunnery on the Mount of Olives.*

203

204

205

207

RYMIS OFFERENS EXAVDITVS EST PRO SVA REVERENTIA

All around Jerusalem are shrines associated with the life of Jesus and the Apostles, and some of these are very old.

The Monastery of the Cross, in the Valley of the Cross, is one of the oldest religious structures in the Holy Land that still remains intact and in use. Nestling in a pleasant valley between the residential suburb of Rehavia and the modern Israel Museum, it owes its name to the tradition that the tree from which the cross of Jesus was cut grew on this spot. It is not known who built the original shrine, which has been variously attributed to Emperor Constantine and his mother Helena, and to the

5th-century Georgian (Caucasian) King Tatian. In any event, during the high Middle Ages it was already attracting pilgrims from the Christian world. Owned by the Greek Orthodox Church, the monastery looks like a medieval fortress.

The Russian Compound, built in the 19th century to accommodate Russian pilgrims to the Holy Land, which included a hospice, a hospital, a church and a convent, is in the centre of the new city, and lends it a stately aspect with its gracious proportions.

Marking the site of the Garden of Gethsemane, where Jesus spent his last night on earth, stands the modern Church of All Nations,

whose pediment is decorated with a brilliant mosaic depicting Jesus as the link between Man and his Creator, with the whole of mankind looking up to him with hope. Behind it rises one of the most surprising structures of Jerusalem — the Russian Church of Mary Magdalene, with its cream-coloured arches and golden onion domes — as if a piece of the snow-bound landscape of Russia was by magic transplanted to the Middle East...

205. The Monastery of the Cross.
206. The cathedral in the Russian Compound.
207. The Church of Ascension.
208. View over the Church of All Nations to the Russian Magdalene Church.

The Dome of the Rock, with its shining golden cupola and exquisite blue base, rests like a jewel on the heart of Jerusalem. Nearby, at the southeastern corner of the Mount, the silver dome of El Aqsa shimmers in the sunshine.

The Temple Mount, on which these shrines stand, has a recorded history of nearly 4,000 years. It is traditionally identified as Mount Moriah, where Isaac was to be sacrificed by Abraham to God. King David captured it from the Jebusites, and it was here that the

209

210

First and Second Jewish Temples stood.

The *Haram esh Sharif* (the Noble Temple), as the Temple Mount is called in Arabic, was a scene of desolation at the end of the 7th century, when the Umayyad Caliph Abd el-Malik had the Dome of the Rock built upon it. The building shelters the rock on which, according to Jewish tradition, the Holy Ark was laid. The Moslems also believe that it was from here that Mohammed ascended to heaven. The Dome of the Rock is sometimes mistakenly called the Mosque of Omar, after the caliph in whose reign the Holy Land was brought under Moslem rule.

The Mosque of El Aqsa is the third most sacred shrine in Islam.

209. *An Arab sun-dial set into the Arcade of the Scales at the southern entrance to the Dome of the Rock.*
210. *A lovely view of the Dome of the Rock with the Mount of Olives above.*
211. *The fountain in Muristan Square.*
212. *The Mameluke dome of the Moslem shrine, Sabil Qaitbay.*
213. *Arab worshippers on their way to pray.*
214. *The El Aqsa Mosque.*

211

212

213

214

215

Its name means "the Farthest", a reference to the "farthest mosque" from Mecca, mentioned in the Koran. It was also constructed at the end of the 7th century. Its spacious, lofty interior recalls the great cathedrals of Christendom. Other Moslem shrines on the Temple Mount include the Mameluke dome of Qaitbay and other small domes and arches built by Moslem princes through the ages.

The character of Jerusalem can never be summed up in a phrase. It is the most multifarious city, with the widest variety of styles, architectural and human.

The Old City retains the leisurely rhythm of the East — old men sitting on small stools outside the cafés smoke *narghiles*, gazing around them in stately calm; the bargaining in the *souk* goes on peacefully, without a rush; craftsmen work at their traditional hand-

216

icrafts with painstaking care. The
eyes feast on the colourful scene —
the silver and gold of jewellery,
the oriental carpets, inlaid wood-
work from Bethlehem, Beduin
robes, embroidered Arab dresses,
glazed Armenian ceramics, embossed leathers . . . The smells of the
market range from the aromas of
spices and perfumes — jasmine and
orange blossom — to the tempting
smells of Turkish coffee and sweet
pastries, roasting *shishkebab* and
freshly-baked bread. The streets,
or rather alleys, are usually special-
ized markets: in one the shops sell
nothing but sheepskins and leather-
ware, in another, spices and scents,
still another has nothing but
jewellery on display, or magnificent hammered and engraved silver
and copper trays and jugs from
Persia. Outside the city walls, there
is a sheep market every Friday. It
is a scene reminiscent of Bible
illustrations, strangely incongruous
beside the busy highway.

*215/216/219. A wide array of wares
is on display in the markets of the Old
City of Jerusalem. Beaten brass and
silverware, embroidered dresses, rugs and
sheepskin coats are among the most
popular attractions of the souk.
217. The sheep market near the northeastern corner of the city walls.
218. Arabs sit outside the Old City
walls.*

217

218

219

The new city of Jerusalem began to develop in the 1860s, when a group of orthodox Jews left the Jewish Quarter inside the Old City and established a small quarter off the Jaffa Road, some distance from the walls. A hundred years later the new city numbered a quarter of a million inhabitants, and had spread as far as the eye can see.

One of the most prominent landmarks in the new city, even in this day of high-rise buildings, is the Y.M.C.A. tower. Begun in 1928, the Y.M.C.A. complex was completed five years later. Its designer was Q. L. Harmon, whose best-known creation was the Empire State Building in New York. Its decoration, however, was the work of local artists.

Today the Y.M.C.A. serves as a community centre for all the inhabitants of Jerusalem. It has sports facilities, including a swimming pool — the first to be built in Jerusalem — as well as a library, an archaeological exhibition and accommodation for guests. From the top of the tower a magnificient panorama of Jerusalem and its environs spreads before the visitor. The top of the tower is decorated with figures of seraphim: "Above him stood the seraphim, each one had six wings" (Isa. 6:2).

When you see the panorama of Jerusalem from the Mount of Olives, the Old City and the New seem to coalesce into a whole, with a special character of its own. In the foreground, between the ridge and the Old City, lies the ancient Jewish cemetery, with olive trees interspersed among the tombstones which reach right up to the city walls and the Gates of Mercy.

Behind the tawny, crenellated walls, built by the conquering Ottoman Turks in the 16th century, the raised platform of the Temple Mount displays its mosques, domes and arches, punctuated by the dark green "candles" of the cypresses. Further away lies the Old City, its houses huddled close together, their stone walls topped with rust-red roofs or small domes, here and there a church steeple rising out of the huddle. The new city lies beyond and around the old, with its clearly-defined modern housing estates, and here and there a high-rise hotel or office block. The effect is rather like looking through time — from the ancient era to the modern, across the intervening ages.

*220/221. Jerusalem: a mixture of old and new — the tall modern buildings of the new city and the ageless structures of the Old City.*

222

223

224

Leaving Jerusalem on the way to Jericho, on the other side of the Mount of Olives, a ruined Crusader tower rises over a small Arab village, surrounded by orchards. This is the biblical Bethany, called Al-Azariya (an Arabic corruption of the name "Lazarus"). It was here that Mary and Martha lived with their brother Lazarus, who died and was resurrected by Jesus.

The grotto on the site of the tomb of Lazarus, like so many other Christian sites in the Holy Land, was made into a shrine in the 4th century AD. In the course of the centuries several churches were built in the vicinity, but most of them no longer exist. A fortified monastery was built in the 12th century by Queen Melisande, but after the fall of the Crusader kingdom it was abandoned and destroyed. Only the tower survived, and it is a prominent landmark to this day.

In the 16th century the Moslem rulers built a mosque over the grotto, but about a hundred years later Christians were allowed to open another entrance to the tomb, so as to be able to pray in it. It is a dark and damp cavern, and the caretaker has to light your way down the 27 rather slippery steps that lead into it.

Since the 19th century there has been considerable development of Christian institutions in the vicinity of Bethany, including an Anglican refugee centre, a Benedictine monastery, a Greek Orthodox school and monastery and a Russian Orthodox school. The Catholic Church bought the land near the 16th-century mosque and had the place excavated by archaeologists over a long period. Some remains of old churches were discovered

in the process. In 1952 the Franciscan Church of St Lazarus was
built on the site, and two years later
the minaret of the mosque was
restored.

In 1964 Pope Paul VI visited the
Holy Land, and on this occasion
King Hussein of Jordan offered the
Pontiff a piece of land on a rocky
hill a little further along the Jericho
road. When this fact became known,
the villagers of Bethany-Azariya
hurriedly erected a mosque on the
property, thus preventing the con-
summation of the gift . . . The new
mosque is known by the rather pi-
quant name of The Pope's Mosque.

*222. The village of Al-Azariya viewed
from above St. Lazarus' Tomb.*
*223. Crusader ruins of a fortified
monastery beside a church in Bethany.*
*224/225. The aura of ancient times con-
tinues to pervade the village.*
*226. Milestone standing in the village.*
*227. Entrance to St. Lazarus' Tomb.*
*228. (overleaf) Ancient plowing methods
are still employed in the Holy Land.*

Jesus' parable, showing how a member of a sect considered lowly and dubious acted with greater compassion than the so-called Men of God, captured the imagination of generations to come. To commemorate it, the Byzantines built a church on a hill overlooking the road to Jericho and the Crusaders later added a fortress. The Mamelukes built a *khan* (inn) and the Ottoman Turks a police station. This station was bombed by the British in World War I, fortified by them against a German invasion during World War II, captured by the Jordanian Arab Legion in 1948 and by the Israeli army in 1967. But despite its stormy history, the site remains a vivid backdrop for one of the most moving tales of compassion ever told.

One of the most vivid parables in the Scriptures is that of the Good Samaritan. "And Jesus answering said: 'A certain man went down from Jerusalem to Jericho, and fell among thieves, which stripped him of his raiment and wounded him and departed, leaving him half dead'" (Luke 10:30).

The road from Jerusalem to Jericho is one of the most desolate in the world and, even in ancient times, when the hillsides were not as bare as they are now, it was undoubtedly a bad place in which to "fall among thieves". The road plunges steeply from the crest of the Judaean mountain range to the deepest gash in the surface of the earth. The sun beats down and a cry may echo among the rocks, eliciting no response.

*229. Inn of the Good Samaritan off the Jerusalem-Jericho road.*
*230. A burst of spring flowers.*
*231. A signpost on the Jerusalem-Jericho road marks the sea-level.*
*232. The Judaean desert as seen through the vault of a Byzantine church.*
*233. End of the aqueduct of Wadi Kelt near Jericho.*
*234. Shelled signpost on road to Jericho, symbolizing the area's stormy history.*

سطح البحر

פני ה‏'‏ם
SEA LEVEL

On the plain that overlooks Jericho, not far from the Inn of the Good Samaritan, are the ruins of a Byzantine church. With not a single source of water in the vicinity, a more inhospitable site for a place of worship would be hard to imagine, attesting to the fierce determination of the early Christians who wished to commemorate every event in the life of Christ.

The number of churches constructed reached a peak in the 6th century AD. In Palestine and Syria alone, well over 200 churches have been discovered dating from that period, almost all of the classical basilica type. However, these churches were usually at the centre of a town, and it is rare to find them in such isolated places as the Plain of Adummim. External decoration was limited to porticoes and lintels on these buildings. Their interiors, however, were breathtaking, with beautiful mosaic floors, wall frescoes, and sculptured columns. Some of the church walls were even covered with glass mosaics. Most of the inscriptions found are in Greek, but there are also exam-

232

ples of Syriac, Coptic, Latin and Aramaic inscriptions. Little is left of the church on the Plain of Adummim, but the vista of the Judaean desert is magnificent, and no doubt it inspired the early Christians who built the church in the middle of the wilderness.

Elsewhere in the desert east of Jerusalem, water is usually brought in by ingenious devices.

The aqueduct of Wadi Kelt, bringing water to the vicinity of Jericho, is a reconstruction of an ancient aqueduct built by Herod the Great, whose winter palace was nearby. At the monastery of St. Chariton in Ein Fara, a modern pump carries water to the solitary monk who lives there, replacing an ancient channel which has since dried up.

233

234

235

Lying near an ancient crossroads on the way from Jerusalem to Jericho, about 300 metres below sea-level, is an old tomb which the Moslems believe to be that of Moses. It is not clear how this tradition came about, as the Bible plainly describes the Servant of the Lord dying in the land of Moab, east of the Jordan, in sight of the Promised Land, and "no man knoweth of his sepulchre unto this day" (Deut. 34:7).

To compound the confusion, many Moslems believe it is not Moses, but Moses' father-in-law Jethro, who is buried here. They also believe that it was Jethro, not Joshua, who led the Children of Israel into the Promised Land after Moses' death.

The reputation of Nebi Musa as a holy place goes back to the Middle Ages. Every year, in springtime, the place teems with Moslem pilgrims who come from all around and spend several days feasting and celebrating the memory of the first prophet. The season for the pilgrimage coincides with the Jewish feast of Passover, as both of them commemorate the exodus of the Children of Israel from Egypt's "house of bondage".

There are several structures in the place, surrounded by a high wall with a single gate facing west. The main edifice has several chambers and vaulted porticoes. There is also a mosque surrounded by domes and a minaret; the tomb is inside the mosque. The principal structure was built in the reign of Dhar al-Baibars, the Mameluke King of Egypt, in 1290, and the minaret, according to Mujir a-Din, was built in 1500.

Like all Moslem shrines and places of worship, this is entirely free of figurative decorations, using only the qualities of the materials themselves to adorn the structure, relieved here and there by the addition of ornamental tiles, bearing floral patterns or Koranic inscriptions.

The springtime festivities are very popular and gay. After prayers at the Temple Mount shrines, the Moslem pilgrims take the Jerusa-

236

lem-Jericho road, turning off it near the Dead Sea to reach Nebi Musa in the afternoon. Leading the parade are persons carrying banners bearing verses from the Koran. Music fills the air, played on traditional instruments, such as drums, cymbals and flutes. Whereas in the past the journey was made on horse- or camel-back, nowadays it is chiefly the automobile which carries the pilgrims to Nebi Musa. Buses running from Jerusalem to Jericho at this time of the year are often filled with such pilgrims, dressed in their traditional costume. Loaded with food for the celebration, they are taken to the site despite the fact that it is off the scheduled route. The gaunt, fortress-like compound, seemingly unrelated to the everyday world, becomes the focus of colourful assemblies and noisy festivity.

The main cemetery serving the Beduin tribes of the region lies around the Nebi Musa compound. Here also lie buried many distinguished pilgrims who came to find their eternal rest in this holy place. A popular belief exists that burial near the tomb of a saintly person imparts the souls of the departed with some of the holiness that lingers in the place. An ordinary person who has the good fortune to lie beside a holy one may be reincarnated as a holy person himself. Also nearby is the tomb of Sitna Aiesha, the Prophet Mohammed's beloved concubine.

The Judaean desert around Nebi Musa has for centuries been haunted by marauders, shepherds, hermits and monks. In the early centuries of this era, many devout pilgrims came to the Holy Land and remained as monks or hermits. The Judaean desert, with its profound religious associations, attracted many of these mystics, who settled in its caves and ruins, to worship God in solitude and await the Second Coming.

*235. View of the Moslem shrine Nebi Musa, the legendary tomb of Moses.*
*236. Cupola of the church of Nebi Musa.*
*237. Pillared entrance-way to the tomb.*
*238. Minaret of the sanctuary.*
*239. Arabic inscription above the vaulted entrance to the tomb.*

A deep, gaping gash in the earth, the riverbed of Wadi Kelt collects water from three streams, flowing from the Beth-El mountains north of Jerusalem downwards and eastwards in the direction of Jericho, and culminating in a chasm near the ruins of Herod's winter palace.

It was here, following in the footsteps of the Prophet Elijah, that the first Christian hermits chose to settle in Byzantine times. St George of Coziba inhabited a cave in the gorge and was subsequently joined by other anchorites. The monastery that stands today was originally founded in the 6th century and was

240

241 WADI KELT AND THE MONASTERY OF ST GEORGE

reconstructed by Crusaders following its destruction by the Persians. Known as St George's, or the Blue Monastery, its chapel holds numerous icons and frescoes. The structure, which clings precariously to the canyon wall not far from Jericho, is believed to stand on the site of a 4th-century synagogue.

*240. Arab woman watering goats in the desert near Jericho.*
*241. The thin duct cut into the rock at Wadi Kelt carries water from the mountains of Beth-El down to Jericho.*
*242. Altar in the church of Quarantal, believed to be the spot where Jesus fasted for 40 days.*
*243. St. George's Monastery at Wadi Kelt.*

242

243

The Gospels according to Matthew and Luke describe how the devil took Jesus into the wilderness to tempt him. "And the devil, taking him up into a high mountain, shewed unto him all the kingdoms of the world in a moment of time . . . And Jesus answered and said unto him: 'Get thee behind me, Satan!'" (Luke 4:5-8).

Tradition identifies this mountain, overlooking the oasis of Jericho, as the one on which the Temptation took place. It was first settled in the 4th century by Greek monks, led by St Hariton. They lived in the caves in the vicinity, and built a monastery on the ruins of the Hasmonaean Dagon fortress. When the Persians invaded the Holy Land in the 7th century the monastery was destroyed and the community dispersed.

In the 12th century the Crusaders attempted to resettle the place, and the Knights Templar built a small fort on the hill top. The small community lived by working in the sugar mill in Jericho, which was owned by the Greek Patriarchate in Jerusalem. In the 19th century some Ethiopian monks lived in the ruins.

In 1875 the Russian Orthodox Church began to construct the present monastery, completing it in 1905. In 1935 a modern church was begun, but remained unfinished. Perched on the steep mountainside, the monastery appears to be a part of it.

The name of this monastery is Quarantal, which comes from *quarante*, forty, commemorating the 40 days and nights that Jesus fasted in the desert. Inside the monastery itself there is a stone on which it is believed that Jesus sat during the first Temptation. There are also rare medieval art treasures and religious objects in the monastery, as in others like it in the Judaean desert.

244. The tower of Quarantal.
245. The monastery of Quarantal clings to the sheer mountainside.
246. The site as seen from Jericho.
247. A narrow corridor separates the monastery and the mountain rock.

248

The cluster of palm trees which marks a rich oasis in the midst of the arid Judaean desert can almost be mistaken for a mirage. In fact, according to biblical tradition, it was a miracle which brought fresh water to the ancient barren town of Jericho: "And the men of the city said unto Elisha, 'Behold, I pray thee, the situation of the city is pleasant . . . but the water is naught and the ground barren'. And he said: 'Bring me a new cruse and put salt therein'. . . And he went forth unto the spring of the waters, and cast the salt therein, and said, 'Thus saith the Lord, I have healed these waters. There shall not be from thence any more death or barren land'" (II Kgs. 2: 19-22). To this day, the life-source of the city flows from the Spring

249

of Elisha (*Ein al-Sultan* in Arabic), joined by the waters of the more distant Ein Doch.

Ancient Jericho is considered one of the oldest cities in the world — perhaps the very oldest. In Tell al-Sultan, two kilometres away from modern Jericho, and rising some 20 metres above the surrounding plain, was unearthed a history of habitation going back to the prehistoric Natufian culture of the 11th-9th millennia BC. At that time the area was populated by semi-nomadic cult-worshippers who lived in huts. An early Neolithic culture has been recorded from *c*. 8000 BC, when some 2,000 inhabitants lived in the area, protected by fortifications. This sedentary population grew into a flourishing urban community in the 7th millennium. Archaeologists have uncovered square-cut holes deep in the earth, which apparently served as dwelling-places. Pottery shards from this period, many characterized by reddish ornamentation, appear to be the earliest examples of the art.

But the tell at Jericho reveals much more information of interest; destruction, earthquakes, prehistory merging with recorded history — all these are traceable in the archaeological finds. Small, irregularly-shaped rooms which were apparently used to store large quantities of grain have been dated as Middle Bronze Age, indicating that Jericho was then inhabited by nomadic shepherds. At that time defensive walls were rebuilt around the town. The Hyksos brought about a cultural awakening, but their civilization came to a violent end in 1560 BC. The Canaanite period began soon afterwards, the traditional story of its abrupt and

total destruction by the Israelites in 1220 BC is well-known to all who are familiar with the dramatic events in the Bible: "And the seventh day shall ye compass the city seven times, and the priests shall blow with their trumpets. And it shall come to pass, that when they make a long blast with the ram's horn, and . . . all the people shall shout with a great shout: . . . the wall of the city shall fall down flat' " (Josh. 6:1-5).

Archaeological finds have partially substantiated the Old Testament account — sections of the fallen wall have been unearthed, bearing no traces of battle damage.

Jericho was a thriving city in ancient times. Developed on a grand scale by Herod, it was destroyed by the Romans when they suppressed the first Jewish revolt (AD 66-70). However, Emperor Hadrian had it rebuilt, and during the Byzantine period the city was inhabited. Eusebius mentions Jericho as a thriving city, and it is shown on the Madaba Map (6th century AD). In the seventh century a large synagogue was built there, whose handsome mosaic floor has been uncovered. After the Arab conquest Jericho became an important winter resort for the ruling classes. Today the city of Jericho retains its peaceful character of a desert town, surrounding the lush oasis which makes its existence possible.

250

251

252

248. *Sunlight streams through the leaves and red blossoms of the acacia tree.*
249. *Rows of wind-swept palm trees have shaded the city of Jericho since biblical days.*
250/251. *The waters of Elisha's Spring, the city's life-source today as in ancient times.*
252. *Rock tower of ancient Jericho uncovered in archaeological excavations at Tell al-Sultan.*

Atop a small hill in the parched stillness of the Judaean desert, northwest of Jericho, not far from a modern Arab café, stand the remains of a 6th-century synagogue and its adjoining courtyard, which were discovered accidentally during the last days of World War I. A Turkish shell fired at a nearby British fort ripped open the earth, exposing the ruins and the synagogue's elaborate mosaic floor. Archaeological excavations soon followed and confirmed the tradition that this hill was the site of the biblical Na'aran (Josh. 16:7; I Chr. 7:28).

The most striking feature of the synagogue at Na'aran is its mosaic pavement. While most of the floor is in black and white stone, the centre aisle of the hall contains elaborate coloured designs, framed by a broad border and measuring 5 by 15 metres in area. This detailed stone "carpet" can be said to be divided into three unequal parts: the lowermost half is composed of geometric patterns (basically, intertwining circular and hexagonal designs) framing pictures of animals and bounded by lotus blossoms. A variety of fruits — figs, carobs and

grapes among them — appear in the half circles surrounding the border in this portion of the floor.

The section above this intricate geometric design is decorated with the signs of the zodiac, with symbols of the four seasons appearing in the corners. Many of the astrological signs were completely gouged out, probably by Jewish zealots of a later period, who opposed the depiction of human and animal images. The value they ascribed to the written word is shown by the fact that the Hebrew letters identifying the zodiac illustrations were left intact.

The top portion of the coloured mosaic depicts the Holy Ark flanked by a pair of candelabra (*menorahs*) hanging from their outer branches, and two lions standing below. Beneath the ark is the damaged image of a man, his hands lifted in prayer. A number of Hebrew inscriptions are found near this figure.

In the aisles of the hall, on either side of the coloured mosaic, are black and white geometric patterns as well as representations of birds and animals. Two gazelles against a background of flowers decorate the floor near the main entrance.

References to Na'aran in the works of Josephus and Eusebius indicate a continued Jewish presence there, from the Israelite era until the destruction of the synagogue in the early part of the 7th century AD.

*253. This Byzantine aqueduct and bridge are situated to the left of the Na'aran synagogue site (not shown).*
*254/255. Part of the mosaic pavement at Na'aran, accidentally discovered in the beginning of the century. Shown here are the pair of gazelles which grace the main entrance-way to the synagogue hall.*

254

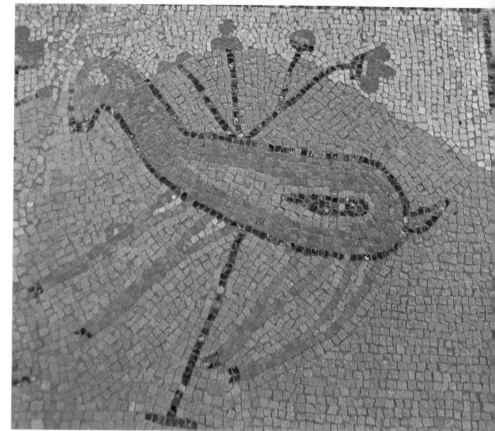
255

256

The vicinity of Jericho was always a famous winter resort of princes in the Holy Land. The Hasmonaean rulers built themselves winter palaces here, to enjoy a warm respite from the raw winter of Jerusalem; Herod followed in their footsteps but, being the greater builder, did it much more grandly; he was followed by the Romans, who appreciated the healthy, dry, warm winters of the Jericho oasis and its environs. But it was the Moslem Umayyad Caliph Hisham in the 8th century, who built the most exquisite palace in this place, much of which survives to this day.

The palace was badly damaged in an earthquake, soon after, and was never inhabited at all.

Known locally as Hirbet al-Mafjir, it follows the architectural design favoured by the Umayyads — a great courtyard surrounded by halls and rooms, with towers at the corners and in the middle of the outer walls. The interior of the palace is extraordinarily ornate and lavish, with a variety of plaster, stone and mosaic ornamentation. At this time the Moslem prohibition of all pictorial representation of living things was not yet enforced, and the palace contained statues depicting women — dancers or concubines — a splendid ceiling ornamented with intricate plaster mouldings depicting human heads, fruit and leaves (it is kept at the Rockefeller Museum in Jerusalem for protection), and a frieze of partridges, also in plaster, that formed a border along the top of the audience hall. The floor of the audience hall is decorated with a beautiful mosaic in green, gold and brown tones, showing three gazelles eating the leaves of a tree and a lion pouncing on one of them. A tremendous star-shaped window in carved stone now stands in the middle of the courtyard.

256. *Detail of carved stone at the entrance gate of the palace.*
257. *Star-shaped window in carved stone fitted into the second storey of the palace.*
258. *Remains of columns that lined the entrance gate of the palace.*
259. *The base of one of the columns.*
260. *The floor of the audience hall, in vivid green, gold and brown mosaic.*
261. *The pool was surrounded by a highly ornate wall.*

257

258

117

259

260

261

262

263

On the eastern horizon lie the mountains of Moab; on the west, the Judaean Hills. Here, on the bank of the Jordan River, in the shallow waters near Jericho, Jesus was baptized and "lo, the heavens were opened unto him, and he saw the Spirit of God descending like a dove, and lighting upon him" (Matt. 3:16). This tranquil site, flanked by bramble patches and date palms and known as El Maghtas, has at-tracted pilgrims seeking immersion and baptism since the very beginnings of Christianity.

The holiness of El Maghtas has been commemorated by many religious shrines. In the 5th century, a Byzantine basilica (named after St John the Baptist) was erected on the site. It was destroyed by the invading Persians in 614, and rebuilt in 1128 by the Byzantine Emperor Manuel Comnenus I.

Reconstructed anew in 1882, the monastery's present form dates from 1954, when the Greek Orthodox Patriarchate in Jerusalem had it renovated. Nowadays there are two monks living in the place and looking after it. The site being 365 metres below sea-level, this is the lowest monastic compound in existence. In the 19th century, its community of monks in the spring of every year baptized pilgrims visiting the Holy Land. The Turkish government provided them with protection from zealous Moslems who returned at this time from celebrations at nearby Nebi Musa in the Judaean desert. The monastery, together with an altar added by the Catholics in 1933, was damaged by an earthquake in 1956; both have been restored.

In Arabic, the Greek monastery of St John is known as *Qasr el-Yahud*, the Castle of the Jews. This is explained by the tradition which identifies the spot as the shallow crossing where Joshua led the Children of Israel into the Land of Canaan. Indeed, this section of the Jordan River is so narrow that it is hardly more than a stream in summer.

264

119

Coptic, Armenian, Rumanian, Franciscan, Syrian and Ethiopian churches also commemorate the biblical baptism. Most of them are located across the river, in the Kingdom of Jordan; a few are on the western bank of the river. One of those is the Monastery of the Holy Trinity, built in 1933 by Empress Menen, the deeply religious consort of Ethiopian Emperor Haile Selassie I. An interesting story is told about the Abyssinian hermit, Abba Amde Michael, whose tomb is within the monastery walls. During World War I, when the Turks were fighting British-led Arab forces in the region, the hermit was moved to Jerusalem; by the following morning, however, he was back in his cell on the Jordan, and never left it again.

The land purchased by Empress Menen from the monastery had been occupied by Ethiopian hermits for centuries; in fact, this African orthodox Christian community has resided in the Holy Land since the 4th century AD, when its members came on foot via Sudan and Egypt. Of the many Christian denominations established in the Holy Land, the Ethiopians are possibly most strong-rooted in Old Testament beliefs, observing many of the commandments of the Pentateuch. Once a powerful community (in the 17th century they had rights at five holy sites, including the Grotto of David on Mount Zion and the Church of the Nativity in Bethlehem), they now are relegated to the roof of the Church of the Holy Sepulchre in Jerusalem, to small compounds at Bethany, Jericho and Debre Gennet (Amharic for "Mount Paradise") and to the archbishop's residence off the Via Dolorosa. Their

monastery at El Maghtas remains standing, but has been deserted since 1967.

This tranquil place seems uninhabited and still, especially in the heat of the day, when the sun beats down and the air shimmers over the river and its palm-decked banks. At night it comes to life, with a variety of animals, from jackals and hares to swamp cats and multitudes of gerbils. They

are attracted by the water and the rich vegetation beside it. Like the rest of the Jordan Valley, this is also a favourite haunt of migrating birds, which come here in droves in the spring and autumn, on their journeys between Europe and Africa.

262/264. *The convent of St. John.*
263. *Signpost marking the baptismal site.*
265. *Chapel of the Ethiopian monastery.*
266. *The Jordan: site of Jesus' baptism.*

265

266

The starkness of the towering cliffs along the Dead Sea gives the visitor a sense of timelessness. Here, at Qumran, the Dead Sea Scrolls came to light, revealing the existence of a pre-Christian monastic community whose lifestyle conformed in great detail to that of the earliest Christians.

The community at Qumran proved to be a sect of the Essenes, as confirmed by later archaeological finds of the ruins of a Jewish monastery nearby. This ascetic group of Jews, dissatisfied with the rituals of Temple worship, had withdrawn from the greater Jewish community and formed a monastic society in the waste land of the Judaean desert. Here they lived from the 2nd century BC until they fell into the hands of Roman soldiers, who destroyed the Qumran settlement in AD 68, just before the great Jewish revolt.

Being devout scholars, according to Josephus, the Essenes of Qumran spent much of their time copying texts, although they were also ardent believers in manual labour. The manuscripts that have survived, preserved by the dry des-

ert air and undetected by the Romans, were stored in earthenware jugs in neighbouring caves and in the settlement workshop.

The discovery of these historically-invaluable scrolls over 30 years ago was entirely accidental. The story is told that a Beduin shepherd called Mohammed the Wolf was crossing the Judaean desert on his way to Bethlehem, to sell his sheep at the cattle market there for a handsome price. Anxious to elude Arab and British patrols, he took a little-known path that cut through the desolate hills northwest of the Dead Sea. Forced off his chosen route in pursuit of a stray goat, he chanced to toss an idle rock into a nearby cave. The sound of pots breaking inside aroused his surprise and fear, dispelled only upon his return with a companion to find earthen jugs, probably of the type used by the Hebrew matriarchs to gather water. Inside the pots were manuscripts written by members of the monastic community that had lived at Qumran a century before the birth of Christ.

The texts include the Scroll of Isaiah, now exhibited in Jerusalem in the Shrine of the Book at the

Israel Museum, the Manual of Discipline, the Pentateuch, Ecclesiastes and the Copper Scroll, containing an inventory of the Temple treasures hidden on the eve of the Roman onslaught. Many of the other scrolls, deciphered only recently, describe the Essene creed and way of life and suggest a strong resemblance between early Christianity and this form of monastic Judaism.

*267. The caves of Qumran.*
*268. Part of the Habakkuk Commentary from the Dead Sea Scrolls at the Shrine of the Book (Israel Museum).*
*269/270. Remains at the Qumran site.*

271

272

273

As you travel along the western shore of the Dead Sea, the landscape is as bare and as bleak as anywhere on the face of the earth. A smell of sulphur rises from the Sea. Suddenly, like a mirage in the desert, you come upon one of the loveliest sights in the world — a lush oasis hidden among the stony crags, with cascades of water, vineyards, rosebeds and banana groves.

This is En Gedi, the "Fountain of the Kids", where the Shulamite watered her flocks, and King Solomon, escaping from his magnificent palace in Jerusalem, sought her among the vineyards.

A cool cascade of water falls 200 metres from a precipitous crag, draped all around by curtains of green maidenhair fern, golden henbane and the rosy caper shrub. Behind it is a cave, a fit chamber for a naiad, with stalagmites for furniture and moss and fern for bedding. Yet it was in this delicate, romantic setting that one of the most dramatic events in the life of King David took place: "And it came to pass, when Saul was returned from following the Philistines, that it was told him, saying: 'Behold, David is in the wilderness of En Gedi'. Then Saul took three thousand chosen men out of all Israel, and went to seek David and his men upon the rocks of the wild goats. And he came to the sheepcotes by the way, and there was a cave; and Saul went in to cover his feet, and David and his men remained in the sides of the cave . . . Then David arose and cut off the skirt of Saul's robe privily. And it came to pass afterwards that David's heart smote him, because he had cut off Saul's skirt . . . And David said to Saul: 'Wherefore hearest thou men's words, saying, Behold, David seeketh thy hurt?. . . After whom is the king of Israel come out? After whom dost thou pursue? After a dead dog, after a flea?'. . . And Saul lifted up his voice and wept. And he said to David, 'Thou art more righteous than I: for thou hast rewarded me good, whereas I have rewarded thee evil' . . ." (I Sam. 24:1-17).

En Gedi's beauty was famous in biblical times, and served as a poetic metaphor, as for example in the Song of Songs: "My beloved is unto me as a cluster of camphire in the vineyards of En Gedi" (1:14). The freshwater pools must have teemed with fish in ancient times, for the Prophet Ezekiel mentions the fishers of En Gedi (47:10). The oasis belonged to the tribe of Judah, and was an important stronghold and caravanserai in the desert.

In later periods there was a town in En Gedi, where the Romans stationed a garrison. According to Josephus, the town was attacked by zealots, who were fighting against the Roman forces throughout Judaea: "They stripped the houses bare, seized the ripe crops, and brought the loot to Masada". During the Bar Kokhba revolt against the Romans, in the 2nd century AD, En Gedi served the rebels as a military and administrative centre. And in the writings of Eusebius, the Church Father who lived not far from here, we find that during the Roman-Byzantine period there was a flourishing Jewish village here, and rare spices and dates were cultivated in the oasis.

The local tell, which was excavated in the 1960s, stands between the riverbeds of Nahal David and Wadi Ariga. The archaeological evidence shows that the place was first settled in the 7th century BC, which means that in David's time (the 10th century BC) it was still a wilderness, which supports its description as a place of refuge. The tell was found to contain five levels, the oldest of which dates from the Kingdom of Judaea, i.e., the First Temple, (7th-6th centuries BC). Various metal tools, pottery and ovens indicate that workshops had existed here, confirming the description in Josephus, as well

274

as other sources, that En Gedi was a centre for the production of balsam (*opobalsamon* in Greek).

In 1970 a beautiful synagogue floor was discovered, dating from the Byzantine period. It contains a long inscription proscribing people who slander, steal or "reveal the secret of the town to gentiles". The decorative part depicts peacocks eating grapes, and the words "Peace on Israel". After this period En Gedi was abandoned and never rebuilt again.

*271. The waterfall at En Gedi.*
*272. Palm trees at En Gedi.*
*273. Salt mounds float on the surface of the Dead Sea.*
*274. Central medallion of the synagogue pavement (5th-6th century). The birds are depicted in a new, more orthodox abstract approach of the Jewish art in the Byzantine period, breaking away from the naturalistic forms of the earlier Hellenistic period.*
*275. The mosaic pavement. Five inscriptions in Hebrew and Aramaic indicate that here was a predominantly Jewish settlement in the late Byzantine period. The remains of earlier synagogues lie below this pavement.*

275

On the flat top of an isolated mountain, rising 400 metres above the Judaean desert, is the site of one of the most dramatic and symbolic events in Jewish history — an act of voluntary martyrdom performed two thousand years ago, at the time of the Roman destruction of Judaea.

The grim rock of Masada, overlooking the western shore of the Dead Sea, was first fortified by the Hasmonaeans and later considerably enlarged by Herod the Great. At the time of the first Jewish rebellion against Rome, it was an outpost of Jewish zealots who had successfully overpowered Roman guards stationed in the place. The zealots managed to become entrenched in the fortress after Titus destroyed Jerusalem in AD 70. This was not to be tolerated, and the Romans decided to bring down the final Jewish stronghold at whatever cost.

The mission to destroy Masada was entrusted to the Roman Governor, Flavius Silva. Mobilizing the Tenth Legion, as well as thousands of water-bearing prisoners and auxiliary troops, he set up a number of camps around the mountain. He then had a beaten earth ramp built on the western side of the rock, to support a battering ram which would be directed against the fortress walls. On the summit, embattled and unaided, were 960 Jewish men, women and children.

But it took a whole year for the Romans to breach the walls of

*276. Since time immemorial camels have roamed the Judaean desert below the massive natural fortress of Masada. 277. Aerial view of the unbreachable fortress overlooking the Dead Sea. The three levels of the Herodian Northern Palace are clearly seen in the foreground. The winding white line on the left marks the tortuous "snake path".*

276

278

279

280

Masada. The day came when the beleaguered Jews realized that on the following morning heavily-armed soldiers would be storming the summit. The steep surrounding cliffs that had served to protect the little community now prevented escape.

Then the leader of the zealots, Elazar ben Yaïr, addressed his people and exhorted them to die by their own hands rather than allow themselves to be captured by the Romans. As narrated by Josephus, he urged them to "let our wives die before they are abused, and our children before they have tasted of slavery; and after we have slain them, let us bestow that glorious benefit upon one another mutually, and preserve ourselves in freedom, as an excellent funeral monument for us. But first let us destroy our money and the fortress by fire: for I am well assured that this will be a great grief to the Romans, that they shall not be able to seize upon our bodies, and shall fail of our wealth also: and let us spare nothing but our provisions; for they will be a testimonial when we are dead that we were not subdued for want of necessaries; but that, according to our original resolution, we have preferred death before slavery".

Ten men were chosen to perform the terrible act. Then one of the ten was called upon to slay his nine companions and finally to take his own life.

When the Roman soldiers, in full battle dress, gained the mountain summit at daybreak, they were met by an absolute hush.

The moving story of Masada has been confirmed and documented by the work of Prof. Yigael Yadin, who, together with an internation-

127

al team of archaeologists and volunteers, carried out the excavations in the mid-1960s. Today, the evidence of these shattering events is visible to all who visit the site.

Yadin and his team uncovered eight archaeological layers, from Chalcolithic caves to a Byzantine chapel, but it is obvious that the Masada restored by Herod and defended by the zealots is of the greatest importance. Extant from Herod's time are the remains of five palaces, three bathhouses, storerooms, giant underground water cisterns, a swimming pool, living quarters and a wall encircling the plateau. By far the most impressive structure is the triple-levelled villa that hangs over the abyss on the northern corner of the plateau, complete with frescoes and double colonnades.

278. *Because of the difficult ascent, excursionists can now use the funicular to get to the top of Masada.*
279. *Here, the Roman Governor, Flavius Silva, set up his camp.*
280. *Ruins at the top of Masada.*
281. *The staircase leading up from the lower terrace.*
282. *Columns of the northern palace on the lower terrace.*
283. *Water conduit leading to the underground cistern.*
284. *The Columbarium at Masada.*

The lowest of the three terraces spreads some 30 metres below the top, and below that there is a sheer drop of hundreds of metres down to the desert floor. In this fantastic place, with the wilderness echoing all around, Herod did not forgo any of the luxuries of a Roman nobleman's existence. A splendid bath was included in the palace, with running hot and cold water, steam rooms and all the other trappings of a pleasure dome. This structure is of great interest — its walls are nearly three metres thick, and so is the brick floor, from which rise 200 narrow columns, supporting the upper floor. This floor was decorated throughout with a handsome, simple black-and-white mosaic, and divided into four apartments.

Herod's residence at Masada was in the western palace. Here the rooms were embellished with brilliantly-coloured mosaics, in floral and geometrical designs. A deep water pool was carved out of the living rock to serve the king in his house. Remains of three staircases attest to the existence of an upper storey in this edifice.

Masada is in the heart of the desert, a harsh land with hardly any rainfall — though in winter it can happen that the canyons suddenly fill with torrential floods that vanish just as suddenly. There are no natural springs in the vicinity either. But Herod's palace lacked for nothing — the water in the wadi to the north was trapped by a dam and conveyed by aqueducts to 12 large reservoirs carved out of the rock. From here it was carried to the cisterns which served the palaces. This water system, which enabled Herod to live in his accustomed luxury, and permitted the embattled Jewish zealots to survive as long as they did, was described in detail by the Roman-Jewish historian Josephus Flavius, in his *Wars of the Jews*.

Why did Herod build this extravagant royal castle in such a desolate area? — Was it to impress his Roman guests with his power, or was Masada meant to serve him as a safe retreat in case of need, as had hap-

286

287

129

pened before he became king, when he had had to take refuge in the nearby fortress of Herodion? This we can only guess at.

In sharp contrast to Herod's extravagance are the crude installations built by the zealots. For example, beside the beautiful mosaic bathroom floor in pink, sky-blue, black and white, installed by Herod, stands a crude, bare wall added by the zealots.

A synagogue and two ritual baths have also been preserved on the site. The former is a rectangular structure with an eastern entrance. Plastered clay benches are located on all four sides and face towards the centre, where the remains of two rows of columns still stand. Dating from the Second Temple period (1st century AD), this is the oldest synagogue found in the Holy Land. It is possible that the building was first used during Herod's reign.

The ritual baths built by the zealots conform exactly to biblical specifications. To provide the pure water required by Jewish ritual law, a cistern for storing the sparse rainwater was built beside the immersion bath.

Perhaps the most dramatic moment in the excavations at Masada was the discovery of 25 skeletons in one of the caves near the summit. A study of the bones by medical and archaeological specialists shows that they conform to descriptions of the zealots.

285. Storerooms utilized by the besieged zealots.
286. Stairway leading to swimming pool.
287. Floor of one of the many baths.
288/289. Wall paintings and capitals found in the Northern Palace.
290. Stone ballista-balls in the Casement of the Scrolls.
291. Huge underground water cistern.

288

289

290

291

The prominent ridge that runs the length of the country from north to south, rising in places as high as 1,000 metres, was of tremendous political significance in ancient times. After the splitting of the Kingdom of Solomon into the two kingdoms of Judaea and Israel, both realms had their capitals in the mountains, and never relinquished them for softer existence in the plains. Jerusalem remained the capital of Judaea and Samaria was the capital of Israel. Despite their relative inaccessibility, both were important cities, the centres of kingdoms powerful and rich enough to tempt the great empires of the Middle East to try and conquer them again and again.

These mountains were not always as bare as they appear today. In ancient times they were covered with forests and thickets, sheltering a variety of wild animals such as leopards, bears and wolves, that all but disappeared in later periods. Some of these forests were cut down by the many conquerors who occupied the land and needed timber for their fortifications and fuel for their armies — Romans, Byzantines, Saracens, Crusaders, Seljuks, Mamelukes and Turks. By the 20th century there were few natural forests left — a few score acres in Samaria and a few on the Carmel. When the trees were cut down the topsoil began to erode, every

winter washing away a little more, until the hills became as gaunt and bare as they are now, except in the places where modern reafforestation has begun to restore the old natural balance.

The population of Samaria has been relatively stable over the ages. Unlike other regions which were almost entirely abandoned, especially in the 15th to 19th centuries, most of the villages of Samaria have been continuously inhabited throughout the years. In the 20th century dramatic events affected the mode of living in Samaria and, indirectly, the agricultural system. The country as a whole began to prosper after the British conquest at the end of World War I, and several villages were consequently rebuilt or greatly developed. In more recent years some of the work force has been attracted to the better income to be found in the cities, and cultivation of the soil has somewhat declined. Intense farming, modern style, enables the Samarian farmer to produce prime strawberries and other delicacies for the local and overseas markets. And so, slowly and subtly, the landscape changes with the mores.

*292. The hills and plains of Samaria.*
*293. A view of the Ramallah-Nablus road cutting through the valleys of Samaria. This landscape was once the scene of Maccabean battles.*

Shiloh — a name to conjure with, a name that brings back the childhood of the race, the innocent faith before the days of temples and palaces.

Once settled in their promised land, "the Children of Israel assembled together in Shiloh and set up the Tabernacle of the congregation there . . ." (Josh. 18:1).

Here, in the first holy place, Joshua cast lots for the division of the land among the tribes, and for the allotment of the cities of the Levites, who would serve all the others before God. It was the centre of worship for a long time, closely linked with the place called Beth-El (the House of God), a little to the south. After the dreadful events of the concubine in Gibeah, as a result of which the Benjamites all but perished at the hands of the other Israelites, a different kind of apportionment took place in Shiloh. Aware that without wives the tribe of Benjamin would be "cut off", the elders of the congregation invited them to abduct the daughters of Shiloh when they came out to dance in the vineyards during a yearly feast of the Lord. And so they did — "and took them wives, according to their number, of them that danced whom they caught" (Judg. 21:23).

A story in a more minor key — but all the more moving for it — connected with Shiloh, is that of Elkanah and his barren wife Hannah, who came there to worship. It was in the sanctuary that the "woman of a sorrowful spirit" vowed to dedicate her son — if one were granted to her — to the service of the Lord. It was here that her prayed-for son Samuel grew up, a youthful aide to the ageing High Priest Eli, and heard God's voice.

294

Later the Ark was taken from the city and carried to Eben-Ezer, where the Children of Israel were waiting to fight the gathering forces of the Philistines. The catastrophe of the loss of the Ark in the battle killed the old priest (I Sam. 4:18). It was also the end of Shiloh's days of greatness, because the Tabernacle was never returned to this place, though its priestly family retained its special importance for a long time to come. It remained a holy place and a symbol of the faith, as the universal popularity of its name indicates.

Traces of the violent consequences of the Philistine conquest were unearthed in the excavations

295

Shiloh (Tell Seilun) has been repeatedly excavated, beginning with a Danish expedition in 1926. It had obviously been a sacred spot for the Moslems at one time, as remains of a mosque and a prayer niche were found on the surface. Just below the surface were found the floors of two churches, quite well preserved. Their mosaics include dedicatory inscriptions and Christian symbols. Beside one of them were found two rooms whose measurements corresponded with those of the ancient tabernacle, as given in the Bible. It is possible that in Byzantine times the site was shown as that of the sanctuary of Eli and Samuel.

296

at Tell Seilun, the place that has been identified as the biblical Shiloh. It was later repopulated and even prospered. During the Roman period Shiloh was highly developed, as archaeological exploration has shown. In the 5th century a fine Byzantine basilica was built there. Shiloh is mentioned by Eusebius and by Jerome

and appears on the famous Madaba Map. Jews continued for many centuries to visit Shiloh and pray there, as we know from the writings of the 14th-century topographer Estori ha-Parhi. In the nearby valley there are a number of Moslem holy places which are also undoubtedly associated with the age-old sanctity of Shiloh.

Evidence found in a small excavation outside the Hellenistic city wall showed that the site was inhabited until the late 12th or early 11th century BC, suggesting that after Shiloh's destruction by the Philistines it was not rebuilt in biblical times, as may be gathered from the words of Jeremiah (7:12).

The site of the sanctuary, however, remains in dispute. Some archaeologists believe that it may have been inside the city, whereas others would seek it in the area south of the mound, along the ancient road, where today are the sanctuaries of Wali Yetim and Wali Sittin, arguing that an open-air sanctuary would most likely have been placed here. In Wali Sittin a lintel, possibly of a synagogue, has been found, showing an amphora between two rosettes and two jars. In the 19th century an ancient sarcophagus, supposedly of Eli the High Priest, was being shown here.

*294/295. Walls of the biblical Shiloh.*
*296. A gnarled tree grows through the roof of the Byzantine church at Shiloh.*
*297. Entrance to the church.*

297

298

The road to Nablus winds through the hills of Samaria, which are covered with sparse vegetation, colouring them a soft greeny-yellow. The country has probably not changed a great deal since the time when the Patriarch Jacob came to settle in it. "And Jacob came to Shalem, a city of Shechem, which is in the land of Canaan, when he came from Padan Aram, and pitched his tent before the city. And he bought a parcel of a field, where he had spread his tent, at the hands of the children of Hamor, Shechem's father, for a hundred pieces of money. And he erected there an altar, and called it El Elohei Israel" (Gen. 33:18-20).

What followed was the disgraceful episode with Dinah, Jacob's only daughter, who was violated by Shechem, son of Hamor, "prince of the country". To avenge their honour, the sons of Jacob tricked the men of the city and then put them all to the sword, "and spoiled their city, because they had defiled their sister". When Jacob protested that he had been put in an impossible position by this act, they answered, "Should he deal with our sister as with a harlot?" (Gen. 34). To this day in this part of the world, a blot on the honour of the family can lead to prolonged vendettas, sometimes lasting through several generations.

Here, according to tradition, Jacob dug a well, which exists to this day. In 1860 the Greek Orthodox Church bought the site, cleaned out the well and began to build a monastery over it. The project was never completed, but enough stands to mark the site from a distance.

Christianity reveres this place for its association with Jesus. It was at this well that Jesus met the old Samaritan woman from Sychar (now called Askar). "Then cometh Jesus to a city of Samaria, which is called Sychar. Now Jacob's well was there. Jesus, therefore, being wearied with his journey, sat thus on the well. Then cometh a woman of Samaria to draw water. Jesus saith unto her. 'Give me to drink'. (For his disciples were gone away to the city to buy meat.) Then saith the woman of Samaria unto him: 'How is it that thou, being a Jew, askest drink of me? For the Jews have no dealings with the Samaritans'. . ." (John 4:5-9).

In the chronicle of the Bordeaux Pilgrim, who visited the Holy Land in AD 333, Jacob's Well is described as a place of baptism. A Byzantine church was built nearby in the 4th century, but the cruciform structure appears to have been destroyed by the Samaritans during their uprising. Emperor Justinian had it rebuilt in the 6th century. By the time the Crusaders arrived in the Holy Land, this church was already half-ruined. The Crusader basilica was built over the well in 1130, but appears

299

to have been in bad shape by the time the Mamelukes drove the Christian knights out of the Holy Land.

A journalist who visited the Holy Land in 1915 described the pervading atmosphere... "We descended into a vault full of shadows and solemnity . . . we saw projecting masonry furnished as an altar with candles, cloths and censers. In the middle of the chamber was an ancient timeworn stone, having a large circular aperture that opened down into the darkness of the earth. With a long exposure, I took a photograph of that old stone, which, according to the inherited knowledge of Christians, Jews and Mohammedans, marks the mouth of the venerable Jacob's Well".

Today, the unfinished Greek Orthodox church stands at Jacob's Well, surrounded by a walled garden. The vaulted room over the well is a typical Greek Orthodox shrine, richly ornamented with icons, gold lamps and candlesticks.

East of the city of Nablus lies the site of ancient Shechem, in a place called Tell al-Balata. It has been excavated by several archaeological missions, and reveals a fascinating history. The excellent location, near the meeting point of three fertile valleys and on the route leading to the sea in the west and to the plateau in the east, was doubtless an important reason for its early settlement. The place is mentioned in Egyptian documents of the 19th century BC, and in the later Execration Texts.

Archaeological investigation has shown that the town already existed in the Middle Bronze Age, which is the time of the Hebrew patriarchs. Remains found from that period include a defensive wall and an Egyptian seal ring of the 12th Dynasty.

Shechem flourished under the Hyksos, the "Shepherd Kings", in the 18th to 16th centuries BC. A double defensive wall was built around it with a triple city gate, and inside a great temple with massive walls and entrance pillars. It was at Shechem that Joshua

*298/299. The city walls of biblical Shechem at Tell al-Balata, east of modern Nablus.*
*300. Fragmented Roman sarcophagi actually situated within a Nablus neighbourhood. The rectangular openings were apparently burial chambers.*

assembled the tribes before his death. After arranging them according to their tribes and clans, Joshua addressed them in the name of the Lord. He recounted to them the tale of the fathers, from Abraham the son of Terah, down to their own generation, which had come into the Promised Land, and swore obedience to God. "So Joshua made a covenant with the people that day, and set them a statute and an ordinance in Shechem" (Josh. 24:25).

The archaeological evidence shows that the town was not devastated by war during this period, so it was probably not conquered but assimilated peacefully by the Israelites. Later, in the days of the Judges, Shechem was the centre of the kingdom of Abimelech, and of the worship of Baal Berith ("Lord of the Covenant", Judg. 9). When Shechem rebelled, Abimelech destroyed it, and the archaeological evidence supports the biblical tale. The glorious days of Shechem came when, after the death of Solomon, the Hebrew kingdom was split in two, Judaea and Israel, with the House of David continuing to rule in Jerusalem, and the Israelite kingdom being ruled by Jeroboam from Shechem. The excavations reveal that during this period Shechem comprised some prosperous quarters, with two-storied houses, and poorer sections. There were also large granaries in the city. The Assyrians ravaged Shechem several times during the 8th and 7th centuries, and the city declined. Only in Hellenistic times did it revive, and become powerful and prosperous again.

It was here that Alexander the Great encamped with his troops in the 4th century BC. The Samar-

301

302

itans settled in the city during its Hellenistic period, but in 107 BC Shechem was destroyed again, this time by the Hasmonaean leader John Hyrcanus, who levelled it to the ground, and the city never recovered. In 72 BC a new city was founded in the vicinity of Shechem and called Neapolis — today's Nablus. In the Madaba Map

of the Holy Land Shechem and Nablus are clearly distinguished, but future generations confused the two, and so it is to this day.

In the year AD 70 Jerusalem was destroyed, Judaea fell and the Romans imposed their direct rule over the country. Two years later Vespasian founded a city on the site of a Samaritan village near the

303

biblical Shechem, and called it Flavia Neapolis. Being in a favourable geographic location and having plenty of water, the city flourished, and so did the extensive territory which was assigned to its rule. It was embellished with handsome Roman temples, an agora and colonnaded streets. Justin Martyr was born here, and Christianity became established in the 2nd century. By 314 Neapolis was the seat of a bishopric.

The most recent discovery in Nablus, made in the first days of 1980, is a Roman theatre. Located on the side of Mount Gerizim, overlooking the Kasbah, Nablus' old quarter, it has an outer wall 5 to 6 metres high, its curve suggesting that it enclosed a considerable space. The seats are being unearthed; it is expected that the amphitheatre, when fully revealed, will serve to illustrate the importance of the Roman city of Neapolis during the heyday of the empire.

When the Arab conquest came, Neapolis retained its name, which was corrupted to Nablus. Under Arab rule the population was mixed — Samaritans, Moslems, Persians and Jews. It was an important city also under the Crusaders, who called it Naples, and made it a royal city, with a palace and a citadel. Thereafter Nablus' fortunes varied — it never enjoyed a powerful status, but neither did it decline.

In modern times the city of Nablus stagnated until about the middle of the 19th century. At this time there were no more than about 10,000 inhabitants, but as the Holy Land became the focus of interest for European powers, several institutions were built in the environs of Nablus, and as a result the population of the town increased and began to prosper. The small, medieval-looking town, with its close huddle of buildings, became inadequate, and new neighbourhoods began to grow on its western side. The Ottoman Turkish government also began to develop the town, adding a town-hall and a garrison, complete with officers' quarters and housing for government officials, as well as a railway station. Later English and German missions built schools and hospitals, and added a hotel, a café and other European amenities, as well as staff houses.

When the British forces conquered the country in 1918, the impact on the small towns of the Holy Land was immediately felt. Greater security and increased economic prosperity affected Nablus favourably, and the city spread outwards. The earthquake of 1927, which devastated many towns and villages in the Holy Land, caused considerable damage in Nablus, but its consequences were on the whole favourable to the city, which received the help it needed to rebuild many of the old houses and add new ones. It also became the administrative centre of the region.

Nowadays Nablus is a thriving city of some 70,000 inhabitants — including the adjoining villages — and is the largest urban centre in Samaria. Its leading industry is soap manufacture, utilizing the local olive oil; its products are sold throughout the Middle East.

304

305

306

*301/302/303/306. Unfinished Greek monastery begun in the 19th century over Jacob's Well in Nablus.*
*304. Entrance to Jacob's Well, where Jesus met the Samaritan woman.*
*305. Interior of the well site.*

307

308

At the eastern entrance to the valley that separates Mounts Gerizim and Ebal, some 230 metres north of Jacob's Well in Nablus, there is a modest landmark which has been revered by all the faiths since the 4th century AD. For, buried in this quiet, almost self-effacing place, are the bones of Joseph, favoured son of the Hebrew patriarch, Jacob: "And the bones of Joseph, which the Children of Israel brought up out of Egypt, buried they in Shechem, in a parcel of ground Jacob bought of the sons of Hamor the father of Shechem for a hundred pieces of silver . . ." (Josh. 24:32).

The authenticity of the site of Joseph's tomb has seldom been questioned, due to the special significance it holds for all the religions. This strong traditional belief was confirmed by the discovery of a nearby tomb and Egyptian relics from 1600-1400 BC, during archaeological excavations undertaken in the area in 1913.

In ancient writings, Joseph's burial site was often confused with Jacob's Well. In fact, it is located between the Well and the ancient tell. The small, domed structure (likened by one traveller to the top of a covered wagon) was restored by Moslems in 1868 and made into a shrine. On the white-plastered walls of its interior, inscriptions in Hebrew and Samaritan can be made out. One inscription states that a certain Egyptian Jew had the tomb repaired in the 18th century. There are small lamps in a recess inside the structure, probably donated by pious Jews in the 18th and 19th centuries. The small pillars at each end of the grave are, according to tradition, the tombs of Manasseh and Ephraim, Joseph's sons, from whom the Samaritans claim descent. The Samaritans have held the site sacred since the 11th century.

Here, then, lie the bones of Joseph, son of Jacob, who, having been sold from his native Canaan into slavery in Egypt, and having risen to the highest position there, lived most of his life in a foreign land. It was not until four centuries after his death that his remains were brought back to his native land, there to be revered for ages to come. Other than the Cave of the Machpelah in Hebron, this is probably the oldest shrine in the country.

In a cave not far from Sebastia, described by the medieval Jewish traveller Benjamin of Tudela as a land gushing with streams and full of "orchards, vineyards and olives", the remains of John the Baptist are believed to be buried. Tradition has it that, after he was beheaded, the Baptist's body was carried by his disciples to the cave where the Hebrew prophets, Obadiah and Elisha, lay buried. The body was purportedly burnt by Julian "the Apostate", so that only the head remained.

In 1099 the Crusaders conquered the former capital of the ancient Kingdom of Israel, and discovered a Greek monastery on the site of the saint's grave. The Frankish knights then erected a magnificent Gothic cathedral, adorned with gold and silver, fine tapestries and art works, which became a major focus of pilgrimage. The ruins of this structure stand to this day. The walls rise to a considerable height from the original foundations of the Byzantine monastery, and piers and columns can be discerned. The tombs can be reached by steps leading from the centre of the church. Some say that not only are the two prophets and St John buried here, but the saint's parents as well —Zachariah and Elizabeth.

The grandeur of the Crusader realm was shortlived. In 1187 Saladin wrested the small village of Sebastia and its outlying area from the Christian knights. The cathe-

309

dral he converted into a mosque, and so it has remained to this day. The present mosque, built in 1893, is located in the eastern part of the medieval church.

Today, most of the inhabitants of the small Arab village of Sebastia work as caretakers on the archaeological site. There is little left to recall the area's former greatness as a major Crusader site, or as the thriving capital of the Israelite kingdom.

*307. Interior of the tomb on the traditional burial site of Joseph.*
*308. Arched entrance to the tomb.*
*309. Mosque minaret seen through the vault of the Crusader cathedral.*
*310. Stairway leading to the cathedral.*
*311. Tomb of John the Baptist. Door leading to a prison under the building.*

310

311

312

The Samaritans are a very ancient people, inhabitants of Samaria, the biblical Kingdom of Israel. They regard themselves as the descendants of the tribes of Ephraim and Manasseh. Nablus, the biblical Shechem, is their centre, being near Mount Gerizim, which is sacred to them. Until the 17th century they had a high priesthood which claimed descent from Aaron, Moses' brother. A version of the Pentateuch — the Five Books of Moses — that differs slightly from the Masoretic one is their sacred text. They hold Moses to have been

God's only prophet, and Mount Gerizim His unique sanctuary. Joshua alone of all other biblical prophets is held in high esteem. God's purpose for mankind, especially Israel, was revealed to the world by Moses, who was "the son of God's house (world)", almost His vice-regent on earth. To him they attribute every word and act which reveals the divine will to mankind. The Ten Commandments are counted as nine by the Samaritans, who have a tenth of their own — the sanctity of Mount Gerizim. There is a rock on Mount Gerizim which they believe marks the site of the sacrifice of Isaac — unlike the Jews who believe that it took place in Jerusalem.

The greatest treasure of the Samaritan community is the so-called "Scroll of Abisha", which is traditionally attributed to Abisha son of Phinehas, the great-grandson of Aaron, who, it is said, wrote it in the 13th year after the conquest of Canaan by the Israelites. Written in gold letters, and wound on two silver rollers, the scroll consists of the Pentateuch (the first five Books of the Bible), in three parallel columns — Hebrew, Aramaic and Arabic. Scholars who have examined the scroll agree that it is not more than about 800 years old.

Most of the other ancient Samaritan texts are written on vellum and bound in book form. The script used by the Samaritans is related to the ancient Hebrew script and closely resembles the cursive Hebrew script of the late Hasmonaean period. (This was subsequently changed in Hebrew when it received what is now its familiar form, the square letters.)

The three languages of the Scroll of Abisha (and to some extent, Greek) have been used by the Samaritans for many centuries, though Hebrew predominated in all ritual and literary works. In the Middle Ages a form of poetry, mostly of religious nature, was developed by the Samaritan High Priest of Shechem, Phinehas ben Yussuf. In the 19th century, another Samaritan poet, Phinehas ben Isaac, produced exquisite poetry in Samaritan Hebrew. The Samaritan community in Israel has been actively collecting and publishing this literary heritage.

Samaritan ritual law generally adheres closely to the biblical text, as in the laws of the Sabbath and festivals, and marriage between relatives.

When praying, the Samaritans, like the Jews, cover their heads and wrap themselves in prayer-shawls; like the Moslems, they take off their shoes to enter their house of worship. They do not light fires or travel on the Sabbath.

The principal holy day is Passover, when the Samaritans sacrifice the paschal lamb on Mount Gerizim. On the 14th day of the first

313

*312. Copper Torah scroll case from the Samaritan synagogue in Nablus.*
*313. New Samaritan transcription of the Pentateuch.*
*314. Samaritan priest displays Torah.*

315

month, all members of the community ascend the Mount, to spend the entire week there. They gather around the altar. The High Priest stands on a large stone and reads the story of the Exodus from Egypt while the sheep are being slaughtered according to ritual, one sheep for every family in the community. The meat is later roasted and eaten with bitter herbs and unleavened bread (*matzot*). Other festivals are Pentecost, the

Festival of the Seventh Month, the Day of Atonement — a day of prayer and fasting for every member of the community over the age of one — and Tabernacles.

Like the Jews, the Samaritans circumcise their sons on the eighth day after birth.

The completion of the reading of the Torah is the official beginning of the Samaritans' traditional way of life. It is reminiscent of the Jewish *bar mitzvah* ceremony, but

316

whereas the Jewish ceremony takes place when a boy reaches the age of 13, the Samaritan ceremony is held when the boy has studied the whole Pentateuch. Some do so at the age of six!

Samaritan marriage is a three-stage process. When a Samaritan girl is certain of her choice, she urges the young man to get his parents to ask her parents for her hand. (Occasionally, the young man will do so without the girl's knowledge.) The girl's parents then reply, "We will call the damsel, and enquire at her mouth" (Gen. 24:57). The girl may accept even if her parents are opposed to the match; in that case she appoints a guardian to act on her behalf. The first ceremony is one of consecration (*kiddushim*), and the second, held some time later, is a betrothal ceremony (*erusim*), at which the girl is represented by her father or guardian. The Samaritan High Priest officiates at this ceremony and pronounces the blessings. A bride-price of six silver shekels is paid by the groom's family to the bride's. This is a binding rite, and to sever the connection at this stage is as serious a breach as a divorce. The final ceremony is that of the wedding proper (*nissuim*), which is celebrated with great rejoicing by the community. In recent years many young Samaritan men have married Jewish women, who joined the congregation — thus saving it from near extinction. Today there are some 500 Samaritans in the Holy Land, most of whom live in Nablus, and the rest in the town of Holon near Tel Aviv.

Whereas in Deuteronomy (27: 4-5) the Israelites are enjoined to build an altar on Mount Ebal, after crossing into Canaan, the Samaritan text has Mount Gerizim instead. According to the Samaritans, the sanctity of Gerizim is supreme. They call it Beth-El, the House of God, the place to which God directed Abraham when he left Ur of the Chaldees. According to them, this, rather than Jerusalem, was the object of Abraham's long wanderings, and here the Spirit of God (the *Shekhina*) rested in Joshua's lifetime. This, too, was the place where Jacob chose to build the altar after the horrific events of the murder of the people of Shechem by his sons (Gen. 35:1). Joseph's tomb, say the Samaritans, is proof that the Children of Israel held the place sacred, for would Jacob's favourite son, the Viceroy of Egypt, have been buried in any but the holiest ground?

All over Mount Gerizim there are interesting ancient and medieval remains, including Roman temples, Byzantine churches and early Samaritan synagogues. There is also a 12th-century tomb of a certain Sheikh Ghanem, who was a friend of Saladin. A great deal of history, and even more spiritual fervour, is linked with the peaceful landscape of Mount Gerizim.

*315. Spot used for baptizing in the Byzantine church of St. Mary atop Mount Gerizim.*
*316. View from summit of Mount Gerizim, the spiritual centre of the Samaritans, to Mount Ebal. Ruins can be seen on the hill in the foreground.*
*317. The rock upon which Abraham prepared to offer his son, Isaac, as a sacrifice, according to Samaritan tradition, is on Mount Gerizim and not Mount Moriah.*
*318. Remains of the octagonal Byzantine church of St. Mary.*
*319. The springs which gush on the summit of Mount Gerizim provide water for the flora and fauna.*
*320. According to Samaritan tradition, Moses' tent stood upon this spot.*

317

318

319

320

321

When the Kingdom of Solomon was divided after the wise king's death, Jerusalem remained the capital of Judaea, whereas the Kingdom of Israel, under Jeroboam, had its capital in Shechem, However, when Omri became King of Israel (in 867) he established his capital in the hills of Samaria, in the city of Shomron (Samaria). The House of Omri, of which the Bible has little good to say, was a dynamic dynasty, and gave the little kingdom its finest hour. A powerful and cunning figure, Omri strengthened his kingdom by means of conquest and judicious alliances. He married

his daughter Athaliah to his southern neighbour, King Jehoram of Judaea, and for his son Ahab he obtained the daughter of the King of Tyre, Jezebel.

It was Ahab who made Shomron into a grand and beautiful capital, with an "ivory house" (I Kgs. 22:39). It was a palace decorated with ivory carvings, some of which have been found, testifying to the presence of an advanced and sophisticated culture. Shomron's social iniquities, however, and flagrantly luxurious way of life, angered the Prophet Amos: "I will smite the winter house with the

summer house, and the houses of ivory shall perish..." (Amos 3:15).

The prophecy came true — the Kingdom of Israel was brought down by the Babylonians in 721 BC, and although Shomron recovered and was rebuilt, it was never again to be the capital of a proud and independent kingdom. It became the centre of the Samaritan people, whose descendants, some 500 in number, still live in the area.

In 27 BC Herod the Great, the mightiest builder this country has ever known, began to develop Shomron, which he renamed Sebaste, a Greek form of the name Augustus, in honour of the Roman emperor. After the fall of Judaea and the destruction of the Second Temple in AD 70, the city was renamed Neapolis. It was an important Christian centre in the Byzantine Empire, as may be deduced from the many churches that have been uncovered here, dating from that period. The Crusaders, too, built in Sebastia. Today it is a village with some 200 souls, not far from Shechem (Nablus — mistakenly identified with the ancient Neapolis).

What is left in Sebastia today are mainly the Graeco-Roman remains — an acropolis of impressive dimensions, a Hellenistic tower — a huge, round structure, the oldest one standing — and two rows of columns from the Roman forum, visible from afar. Nearby, an aqueduct has been uncovered, which brought water to the city from the adjacent hills. There are other impressive remains — a theatre from

*321. Tower added to the acropolis walls at Sebastia in the early Hellenistic period.*
*322. Ruins of wall at Sebastia site.*
*323. Roman forum, east of the acropolis, beside the remains of a basilica.*

322

the 3rd century AD, in excellent condition, as well as a stadium, a mausoleum and some tombs from the Roman period.

The wide flight of steps leading up to the temple of Augustus is part of the reconstruction project of Septimius Severus — Herod's temple having been destroyed. But Severus' attempts to revive Sebaste failed, because the country thereabouts was entirely devastated after the crushing of the Bar Kokhba revolt in the 2nd century AD.

In the course of the years many stones from the site of ancient Sebastia have been removed and utilized elsewhere. Some may be seen in the old Nablus railway station or other buildings, where the local authorities did not scruple to incorporate them in their construction projects.

324. Remains of Roman theatre below.
325. A view of the 3rd-century Roman amphitheatre in Sebastia.
326. Architrave with faces in relief.
327. The Roman theatre in Beth-Shean.

Beth-Shean is one of the oldest inhabited sites in the Holy Land. It is mentioned in ancient Egyptian documents from the 15th century BC. It was ruled by the Egyptians, and fortified by Pharaoh Rameses II, who also built a temple there. Later it was a Philistine city, and was influenced by the Aegean culture which the Sea People introduced into the country.

Allotted to the tribe of Issachar, Beth-Shean was actually possessed by the tribe of Manasseh (Josh. 17:

11). However, in the reign of King Saul, it was held by the Philistines, and it was on the walls of Beth-Shean that they hanged the Hebrew king's body (I Sam. 31:10). Later it was one of the principal cities in the realm of King Solomon.

In later centuries, Beth-Shean underwent several transformations. The Hellenistic period saw it renamed Scythopolis, probably because of Scythian mercenary troops who encamped there. Under the Hasmonaean kings the city was rebuilt, and the Romans also enlarged and developed it. Beth-Shean was an important Jewish city during the Mishnaic and Talmudic period, but, in years to come, became a typically Byzantine city, and the capital of a district called *Palestina Secunda*. It was an episcopal seat and had numerous churches.

The excavations at Beth-Shean have been extremely rewarding, with Egyptian, Philistine, Canaanite, Israelite and Jewish, Hellenistic, Roman and Byzantine remains in abundance. The Roman theatre has been partially restored.

Today there is a modern city in Beth-Shean, with light industries and farms all around it. The fertile valley is 120 metres below sea-level and very hot, which somewhat limits its attractions for the modern town-dweller.

The synagogue at Beth-Shean was built in the late 4th or early 5th century, in the form of a basilica.

328. A Greek inscription on a stone at Beth-Shean.
329. Corner of the garden of the museum.
330. Tell with entrance to the Roman theatre in the foreground.
331. Detail of the mosaic floor of the synagogue at Beth-Shean.
332. The decoration of the floor includes the Holy Ark and candelabra.

It was in constant use for a period of about 200 years, attesting to the presence of a Jewish community in the town until the 7th century, when Islam swept through the land. During this period the building was renovated at least once. The mosaic floor is decorated with geometric and floral designs, and includes a representation of the Holy Ark with candelabra on either side, as well as Greek inscriptions.

The Jewish community of Beth-Shean, which flourished from the 2nd century on, was famous for its textile industry, whose wares were exported to other Near Eastern countries.

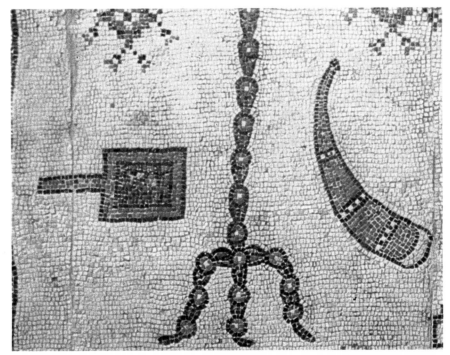

331

Much of what is known today about ancient Jewish art in the Holy Land derives from a remarkable find made while digging an irrigation ditch in the fields of Kibbutz Haftzibah, in the Jezreel Valley. Here the mosaic floor of a 6th-century synagogue was discovered, remains of a basilica-type structure which was built during the Byzantine era.

The surviving mosaic had decorated the nave of the synagogue. Unlike the earlier mosaic floor of the Hammath Tiberias synagogue, the Bet Alfa mosaic is naive, even crude. One panel depicts the near-sacrifice of Isaac by Abraham. The central panel is a gigantic wheel of the zodiac, with a figure resembling the sun-god Helios driving a chariot drawn by four horses.

The four seasons are personified as young women bearing the fruits of their seasons. The third panel shows a seven-branched candelabrum, a ram's horn, a palm frond and citrus fruit.

*333. Bet Alfa synagogue mosaic floor: panels depicting the sacrifice of Isaac by Abraham and a zodiac wheel.*
*334. The zodiac wheel with the sun-god in his chariot in the centre, the twelve signs, and the four seasons, in the corners.*

335

"Belvoir", Beautiful View, that is what the Crusaders called this place, and the view from here is indeed breathtaking. In the northwest — Mount Tabor; in the north — the Sea of Galilee, the Golan Heights and the snowy cap of Mount Hermon; in the south — Mount Gilboa and the foothills of Samaria.

On this promontory in the Jordan Valley, overlooking the vital longitudinal route from Syria to Gaza and Egypt, the Crusaders built a beatiful fortress. Being near their eastern frontier, it also helped guard their kingdom from marauders across the Jordan. In 1168 the Hospitaller Knights purchased its property and for five years

supervised hundreds of workers until they had a superbly-planned fortress, much of which still stands. They were so pleased with it, that in addition to Belvoir they called it La Coquette, which meant in Old French "the pretty one".

The Arabs admired this castle and the royal view it commanded of the surrounding landscape. The Arab historian Abu Shama described it in the following words: "Set amid the stars like an eagle's nest, abode of the moon". And so the Arabic name for the place came to be *Hisn Kaukab*, Star Castle, or *Kaukab al Hawa*, which means the Star of the Winds. The Hebrew name for the place is *Kokhav Ha-Yarden*, which means Star of the Jordan. In ancient times this was a small Galilean Jewish town, where the Romans built a fortress they named Agrippina. Remnants of the Jewish town are to be found in Belvoir, where there are stones embellished with reliefs of traditional Jewish ornaments, such as pomegranates and candelabra, in the Crusader edifice. They must have been found on the site and used by the Frankish knights when they built the fortress. Thus are the eras mingled and run together, until they become like strands woven together into a single tapestry.

After the defeat at the Horns of Hittin, the Crusaders retained only three outposts — Tyre, Safed and Belvoir. Saladin himself led the Saracen armies in their repeated attacks on Belvoir, but, although beleaguered for a year and a half, the Crusaders in the fortress held out, and even made sorties against the besieging forces. Saladin announced throughout the land that the efforts to seize Belvoir were

336

encountering unusual resistance, both because of its massive fortifications, and its "connection with the stars", as indicated by its name . . . Finally, in January 1189, the Moslem engineers succeeded in completing a tunnel from the eastern slope right into the castle keep, which was called the Tower of the Annunciation. By setting fire to the wooden struts in the tunnel the Moslems caused the collapse of both tunnel and keep. But the defenders did not succumb, and the inner fortifications remained firm. Finally, the surviving knights, 50 in number, with some 400 soldiers, surrendered to Saladin. The Saracen general, who was famous for his chivalrous conduct, permitted them to leave with all their belongings, and join their fellow Crusaders in Tyre.

The castle remained more or less intact for 30 years. Then, in 1220, came rumours of a new, daring Crusade being launched, and the ruler of Damascus ordered some of the Crusader forts in the Holy Land to be destroyed. Belvoir was deliberately wrecked, and although in 1240 the Crusaders were once more in possession of it, they did not rebuild it.

The castle measures 140 by 100 metres, and is a first-rate example of a Crusader frontier fortress. The dark basalt stone, in part encrusted with lichen and wreathed with creepers, suggests an everlasting strength. The thickness of the walls and the sheer volume of masonry are almost incredible. There are four towers, one at each corner, as well as the remains of the castle keep which was destroyed by the Saracens. Deep moats guard three sides of the castle, while the fourth is all but inacces-

337

sible due to a smooth, steep slope rising up to it. There was a double gate, with a pierced wall above it, from which boiling oil could be poured on the invaders. Inside the complex there was a central courtyard with a water-well, a dining hall with kitchens, and side galleries. The castle chapel is ruined, but archaeologists who excavated it in this century came upon three exquisite statues, the finest of that period found in the Holy Land. They are now on display at the Rockefeller Museum in Jerusalem.

*335/338. View from vaulted interior of Belvoir fortress.*
*336. General view of the castle ruins.*
*337. The Crusaders re-used stones from older structures.*

338

Travelling south from Tiberias along the Sea of Galilee. About a kilometre-and-a-half away there is a park on the site of the biblical Hammath, mentioned in the Book of Joshua (19:35, 21:32). There are 17 springs here, some 2,000 metres deep, whose water is hot (about 62 degrees centigrade) and rich in various minerals. Their curative properties were famous as far back as the reign of Trajan, when Hammath-Tiberias was a walled city and minted a coin in honour of the springs. The place is extremely popular to this day, attracting local and foreign holiday-makers and people seeking cures for a variety of ailments, from skin diseases to rheumatism.

The 4th-century synagogue of Hammath, discovered in the 1960s, was built in a style resembling that of a Roman basilica, and its mosaic floor shows marked Hellenistic influence. It is one of the most beautiful mosaic floors found in the Middle East, depicting the wheel of the zodiac, with a figure like a sun-god in the centre. The Jewish prohibition of all representation of animal and human figures was not enforced at this time. Later, many similar art works were badly damaged by religious zealots, who gouged out the facial features. Fortunately, the Hammath floor escaped this fate. The zodiac at Hammath is a striking example of mosaic art at its best. The form is the conventional one of that period — two concentric circles within a square. The sun-god figure, however, is unusual and distinctive — he is shown driving a chariot, bearing a whip and an orb in his left hand, while gazing at his raised right hand. Besides the whip are a crescent moon and a star. Each of the 12 signs of the zodiac is shown with its Hebrew name within its section. The four seasons — Summer, Winter, Autumn and Spring — are

341

personified as beautiful women, in the four corners of the square. All the animals and human figures are marked by a natural and sophisticated grace of movement.

In Judaism the zodiac served as a calendar reminding the worshippers at the synagogue of their duties throughout the year. This superb example is the oldest one discovered in the country so far, and is a great attraction with visitors to Tiberias.

339. Remains of Jewish baths of Roman period at Hammath.
340/341. Details of mosaic floor of the synagogue.
342. Central part of mosaic pavement of Hammath-Tiberias synagogue with zodiac signs and names of months in Hebrew.

The southern tip of the Sea of Galilee, at the point where it meets the River Jordan, is a favourite baptismal site. The small fishing boats sailing on the water there and the picnic grounds dotting the shore of the lake create an idyllic atmosphere. This is one of the few places along the Jordan which is accessible to visitors, for much of the river's length forms the border between the nations of Jordan and Israel. Slightly further downstream, the biblical river narrows, cutting through the fields of some of Israel's most prosperous communal farms.

343

344

The Church of St Peter by the Sea of Galilee in Tiberias is a remnant of a Christian community which flourished here in Crusader times. In the 7th century, on the eve of the Arab conquest of the Holy Land, the Christian community of Tiberias was surpassed only by that of Jerusalem. In 723 St Willibald reported "many churches and a synagogue" in Tiberias, and between the 8th and 11th centuries it was an episcopal seat for the Syrian Jacobites and the Greek Church. Tiberias then boasted five churches and a convent. Crusader documents also mention the Hospital of St Julian, the Church of St Lazarus, and the Baths of St Mary.

One of the reasons for the city's popularity in Crusader times may be that the Latins believed Tiberias to be a place where Jesus had lived. In 1106 Abbot Daniel, a Russian monk, described a round church dedicated to St Peter in Tiberias. The existing church has been found to be of Crusader origin, and no one is certain whether this is the church to which Abbot Daniel referred.

The Franciscans acquired the structure in 1847, and had it restored in 1870 and again in 1944. Except for the Franciscan façade, the building is Crusader in style. The masonry is uniform, and the vault and window arches are pointed. The apse, however, instead of the usual semi-circular shape, is angled like the keel of a boat. Some authorities believe the design was intended to commemorate St Peter who was a fisherman on the Sea of Galilee when he met Jesus.

The church of St Peter is best known for its altar-piece, which, however, is no longer in the building, but in the Convent of the Flagellation at the second Station of the Cross in Jerusalem. The Peter and Paul Altar-piece, as the paintings are called, was painted by Friedrich Pacher in south Germany in the 15th century. A series of seven scenes from the lives of the titular saints, they had adorned the altar of a church in Sterzing in southern Tyrol near the Brenner Pass. In the 19th century, when the Tiberias building was a Bavarian mission — before the Franciscans took possession — the paintings were donated to the church here. They adorned the refectory walls of the Franciscan Hospice in Tiberias. During this century they were transferred to Jerusalem, where they are better protected from the elements.

These brilliantly-executed paintings show Peter and Paul as strong patriarchal figures. The two saints are often depicted together by artists, as they were martyred together and share the same feast day.

*343. Pilgrims wading in the Jordan River at a favourite baptismal site.*
*344. Here the Jordan River meets the Sea of Galilee.*
*345. St Peter's Church by the Sea of Galilee in Tiberias.*

345

346

For complete contrast with the bare and awesome vistas of the desert, the landscape around the Sea of Galilee cannot be excelled. It is a green, soft, rather dreamy landscape. In the distance are the violet-blue mountains of Golan, with the snowy cap of Mount Hermon floating, it seems, in the eternal azure. All around are green hills, and, in the centre, a placid, sapphire lake gleaming in the sun. The Hebrew name for the lake is Kinnereth, which comes from the word *kinnor*, meaning lyre, perhaps because of its shape as seen from the mountains of Galilee.

This is a sheltered, fertile valley, watered by the sources of the Jordan — underground springs and the melted snow of the Golan — and warmed by the year-round sunshine. Cereals and fruit trees grow abundantly, cattle graze on the rich grasses, fish abound in the lake. Prehistoric man settled here and flourished, as witnessed by the many Neolithic, Chalcolithic and Bronze Age sites uncovered in the valley.

The city of Tiberias was founded in the second decade of the 1st century AD by Herod Antipas, the son of Herod the Great, and named in honour of the reigning Roman Emperor Tiberius. It enjoyed a measure of autonomy, as cities in the Roman Empire often did, minting its own coins and enacting its own laws; the several religions coexisted peacefully; the principal source of income was fishing.

After preaching in the synagogues of the Galilee, Jesus came down to Gennesaret (the Latinized form of Kinnereth). It was here that he met the fishermen Simon-Peter and Andrew his brother, and James the son of Zebedee and John his brother, and the four followed him to become "fishers of men". It was in the lakeside village of Capernaum that Jesus performed his first miracles and gathered around him his first disciples and followers. Seeing the lake on a summer morning, with a slight mist hovering over its surface, it is not difficult to imagine the miracle of Christ walking upon the water; seeing it on a stormy day, when the usually placid lake becomes dark and threatening, with great waves rising, the miracle of the stilled tempest becomes all the more dramatic.

After the first Jewish revolt and the destruction of Jerusalem, Tiberias became a predominantly Jewish city. In the 2nd century it became the seat of the Sanhedrin and of the Patriarch, who dominated the city, making it the centre of the Jewish population in the Holy Land. The so-called Palestinian (or Jerusalem) Talmud was, in fact, principally compiled in Tiberias. The peaceful coexistence of the religions of the ancient Middle East continued after Constantine the Great established Christianity as the official religion of the Roman Empire. This tolerance continued after the Arab conquest in the 7th century. Designated the capital of the province, Tiberias' importance as a major

347

centre, halfway between Damascus — the seat of the Umayyad dynasty — and Jerusalem, helped it develop economically.

The city did not flourish under Crusader rule, even though Tancred established a principality of Tiberias and built a large basilica in it. During the great battle with Saladin at the Horns of Hittin, Tiberias was nearly destroyed, and then remained desolate for many years. In the 16th century, following the Ottoman conquest, Jews once again began to settle in Tiberias under the leadership of Don Yosef Nassi, the Spanish-Jewish magnate. Ottoman rule favoured the city and it began to revive. The Talmudic associations and the tomb of the great Jewish philosopher Maimonides gave the place a quality of sanctity, which remains to this day. What is known as the Old City of Tiberias is partly Crusader, with Ottoman structures not more than 300 years old. The wall surrounding it dates back to the 12th century.

The 20th century began in Tiberias with a serious outbreak of the plague. The little city was isolated inside its walls, and the only contact it had with the outside world was by telegraph. The *kaimakam* (Ottoman mayor) fled, and there was hunger in the city. The plague raged for 40 days, and its final toll was 650 dead — Christians, Moslems and Jews. The decline that followed did not last, however. In 1905 a railway line was inaugurated, connecting the town of Zemah with Haifa. Tiberians would take a boat to Zemah and from there travel by train to Haifa and other cities of the coast.

After World War I, Tiberias began to develop more rapidly. In the first census held by the British Mandatory Government, 7,000 inhabitants were registered in Tiberias. The first neighbourhood began to spread on the hillsides behind the old walled city. Schools and hospitals were built, to serve not only the local population, but the villages and kibbutzim all around.

Today Tiberias is one the principal tourist attractions in the country. Offering a warm climate in winter, it attracts thousands of visitors from Europe every year. But all year round the physical beauty of the lake and its environs, and the therapeutic qualities of the nearby hot springs, keep the hotels of Tiberias busy. Water sports enthusiasts also frequent the lake, and there are water-ski and sailing clubs to serve them. Today it is a city of some 25,000 inhabitants, and the main urban centre of the region, just as it was when founded in the 1st century AD.

The Sea of Galilee is the main reservoir of fresh water in the Holy Land. It rises naturally every winter and spring, replenished by the streams that swell when the snows of the Hermon melt. Water from the lake is drawn off and carried by pipes to other parts of the country. The purity of the lake is therefore of the utmost importance and efforts are constantly made to safeguard it against pollution.

*346. An elderly Arab couple views the Sea of Galilee while enjoying the cool breeze.*
*347. Fishing is the main means of livelihood in the Tiberias area.*
*348. The famous and delicate St Peter's fish, found only in the fresh waters of the Sea of Galilee.*
*349-351. Boats and fishing gear line the harbour at Tiberias.*

348

349

350

351

North-northwest of the city of Tiberias, on the slopes overlooking the lake, lies the ancient Jewish cemetery. For 1,500 years, from the time when the Sanhedrin had its seat in Tiberias, until the temporary extinction of the Jewish community in the second half of the 17th century, the Jewish dead were buried here, and many were brought from far away for burial in these sanctified precincts.

Travellers in the Holy Land through the ages noted the presence of this special cemetery and described it in their writings. The Arab writer Shams Addin Al Makkadasi in the 10th century

and the Spanish-Jewish traveller Benjamin of Tudela, who came here in the late 12th century, described the place, the latter providing details of burial practices: burial caves were filled with coffins which were placed in rows one on top of the other, and cemented together, for fear of grave robbers. Another medieval traveller, a certain Jacob ben Nathanael, described how the non-Jewish inhabitants of

*352. Entrance to the tomb of Rabbi Meir Ba'al HaNess at Tiberias.*
*353. Exterior of the tomb.*
*354. Religious books and ritual objects are on display and sold to numerous pilgrims visiting the rabbi's tomb.*
*355. Interior of the tomb.*

354

355

356

357

358

Tiberias used to light candles on one of the ancient tombs, believing that the virtue of the deceased would help them in sickness and other troubles. A visitor who mocked them died on the spot, and "the priests and bishops said that this befell him because the dead Jew had been a teacher of Jesus . . .".

In the course of the centuries many of the caves filled up with silt and dirt, especially as floods did not spare the region, and between the 17th and the 19th century there were not enough Jews to maintain the catacombs. Nowadays there are few identifiable tombs left, though many fragments testify to the extent of the burial grounds in ancient times. However, there are several tombs which have been kept up through the ages; among them are the tombs of Rabbi Yohanan ben Zakkai, Rabbi Akiva, Maimonides and Rabbi Yeshaiahu Halevy.

Rabbi Yohanan ben Zakkai was one of the great scholars of the 1st century AD. After the destruction of the Second Temple it was he who re-established the Sanhedrin and the Jewish spiritual centre in the town of Yavneh. According to tradition, his body was brought to Tiberias for burial. His tomb is described repeatedly by Jewish travellers.

Another famous figure in Jewish history is Rabbi Akiva. His life story is one of the best-known and most moving — a simple labourer in the service of a rich Jew by the name of Kalba Savua, he was loved by his master's daughter, Rachel, who prevailed upon him to devote himself to the study of the Law. At the age of forty, Akiva joined the infants in the local rabbi's school and studied, while his wife

163

supported the family, having been disowned by her father. In time, Akiva became one of the leading luminaries of Judaism. During the Bar Kokhba revolt against the Romans, Rabbi Akiva enthusiastically supported the rebel leader, and when the uprising was suppressed, the ancient rabbi and nine of his colleagues, all equally famous and revered, were tortured to death in the stadium of Tiberias.

Maimonides was the greatest Jewish scholar, physician and philosopher of the Middle Ages. He was born in Spain (1135), but lived in Egypt, where he was royal physician to the Sultan. When he died in 1204 he was first buried in Egypt, but his remains were later transferred to Tiberias. His grandson, Rabbi David, called the *Naggid* (president), is also buried here.

Another famous rabbi who is buried here is Yeshaiahu Halevy of Horowitz, who came to Tiberias from central Europe in 1627 and died two years later. A saintly man and a great scholar, his tomb is also greatly revered.

But the best-known tomb in Tiberias, which is marked by two synagogues, is that of Rabbi Meir *Ba'al HaNess*, which means, the Master of the Miracle. As one of the great *Tannaim*, the Jewish rabbis of the 2nd century, fathers of the Talmud, a former pupil of Rabbi Akiva, Rabbi Meir is also a well-loved figure. His cave tomb and its adjoining synagogues attract thousands of pilgrims and visitors every year, and is also revered by the Moslems who live around the lake, as he is believed to be the patron of its fishermen.

The synagogue complex around Rabbi Meir's tomb is one of the most handsome in the Holy Land.

356. *Tombs of Rabbi Yohanan ben Zakkai and of his pupils.*
357. *Tomb believed to be that of Rabbi Moses Hayym Luzzatto, known also as Ramhal, the famous Italian 18th-century kabbalist, writer of ethical works and Hebrew poet, who spent his last years in the Holy Land.*
358. *Maimonides' tomb.*
359. *Pilgrims burn candles in a niche by the tombs of the saintly rabbis.*
360. *Front of Luzzatto's tomb.*
361. *Tomb of Rabbi Akiva.*

359

360

361

362

Magdala was one of the oldest towns in Galilee. Situated on the western shore of the Sea of Galilee, five kilometres north of Tiberias, its name in the Talmud is Migdal Nunaya (The Fisherman's Tower); it is the birthplace of Mary Magdalene (Matt. 27:56, 61). According to the Gospel of St Mark, the town was also visited by Jesus. In the course of the centuries, the place became one of the regular stops on the itineraries of the pilgrims.

According to Josephus Flavius, the Roman-Jewish historian, Emperor Nero gave the town of Magdala to Agrippa II, who later renamed it Taricheae, a Latinized form of the Aramaic word for "drying and salting", a reference to the fishing industry on which the economy of the town rested. During the second Jewish revolt Magdala served the zealots as a base in their fight against the Romans, who in later stages of the revolt besieged the place and conquered it.

After the collapse of the resistance, Magdala became once again a quiet little fishing village on the Sea of Galilee. Today a ruin called Majdal is pointed out as the site of the original town. A small Jewish village called Migdal, which subsists on fruit orchards and dairy farming, is found not far from here, but it is not to be confused with the original biblical village.

363

362. *A splendid wide-spreading Oak tree, not far from Magdala.*
363. *Tomb of Sheikh Mohammad Raslan, revered by the Moslems.*
364. *Interior of the tomb.*
365. *The fortified caves on the slopes of Mount Arbel where the Jewish zealots sought refuge from the soldiers of King Herod the Great in 39 BC.*

364

The stream of Arbel, which is dry in summer, runs east from the village of Aylaboun in the central Galilee to the shore of the Sea of Galilee near Migdal. Rising above the riverbed, not far from the Valley of Kinnereth, is a stony ridge, riddled with caves, whose history is fearsome. The place is associated with the biblical Arbel, mentioned in the Book of Hosea.

During the Hasmonaean revolt against Seleucid Syria in the 2nd century BC, the forces of Judah Maccabee fortified the caves and used them as their camp during their guerilla skirmishes against the Hellenist army. However, the Seleucid general Bacchides succeeded in seizing the slope — or "steps", as it was then called — leading up to the caves, and his forces were able to capture the rebels.

These caves later served the Jewish zealots who rebelled against King Herod the Great in 39 BC. Having taken refuge in these inaccessible caves, they thought they were secure from the King's forces, so long as they kept the slope clear. But the enemy used an original strategy — soldiers were lowered in specially-constructed cages suspended by ropes from the brow of the hill, and, upon reaching the mouths of the fortified caves, used flaming torches to set fire to their entrances, thus burning or choking to death the rebels who hid inside. Those who came out were thrown down to the valley below.

During the great Jewish revolt against the Roman Empire, which broke out in the year AD 66, the caves of Arbel were once again fortified and used by the rebels.

According to *The Life of Flavius Josephus*, it was he who commanded the forces that used these caves as their fortress. But in the end the Jews were defeated throughout the Galilee.

After the destruction of the Second Temple in AD 70, Arbel was settled by priests of the House of Jeshua, and a Jewish community grew there which lasted through the Roman and Byzantine empires into the Middle Ages.

Nowadays the valley of Arbel is still known for its agricultural produce. A cooperative village nearby grows fruit, vegetables and field crops, as well as livestock. The rather forbidding brow of the promontory that dominates the area lends the pastoral scene a touch of the dramatic. The view from its top is magnificent.

366

367

368

It was Saturday, 4 July 1187. The Frankish armies of Guy de Lusignan, the Crusader King of Jerusalem, and of Raymond of Tripoli, his fickle vassal, were advancing towards the village of Hittin, where they hoped to quench the terrible thirst of their long march from Sepphoris. The army of Saladin, the brilliant Saracen general, was sweeping down from Tiberias, which it had just reduced. The Crusader forces were in disarray, chiefly because the princes were at odds with each other, and the King of Jerusalem could not count on the fealty of his vassals. In preparation for this important confrontation, the sacred "True Cross" was brought up from Jerusalem, accompanied by the prior of the Church of the Holy Sepulchre, and the Christian warriors rallied around it.

The clash came when the Frankish cavalry attempted to break through to the springs of Hittin. Exhausted by the midsummer heat, aggravated by their heavy suits of armour, they failed to break through the light Arab cavalry and its relentless shower of arrows. The infantry fled to the summit of one of the "horns", hoping to escape the fate of the cavalry and the smoke of the burning fields. When the "True Cross" was taken by the Saracens, the Crusaders knew they had lost the day. The final scene of the battle, in the Sultan's tent, when Saladin handed the captive Guy de Lusignan a drink of snow-cooled water, has been described in many romantic novels. It was the beginning of the end of the Crusaders' rule in the Holy Land.

A volcanic hill with a curious formation, reminiscent of cow horns, bears the Hebrew name of *Karnei*

*Hittin*, the Horns of Hittin. The village of Hittin is mentioned in ancient Hebrew sources, from the Bible on, as a place where wheat grew (Hebrew, *hittah*).

The place entered history when Saladin, the Ayyubid prince from Egypt, defeated the Crusaders at the Horns of Hittin in 1187. This was the decisive battle that gave victory to the Saracens and marked the decline of the Crusaders' rule in the Holy Land.

The place is remarkable for another reason. Here, at the foot of the mountain, is buried the foremost prophet of the Druze, Nebi Shu'eib, traditionally identified with Jethro, the father-in-law of Moses. Every spring, on the day of Nebi Shu'eib, thousands of Druze from all over the country congregate here to celebrate the founding of their sect. It is a spontaneous celebration, not a religious ritual. Camp fires are lit, old friendships are renewed and the young men hold races and competitions.

The Druze sect originated in the 11th century in Cairo, as an offshoot of Islam. Its tenets are kept secret, transmitted orally from elders to younger people. The former are distinguished by the white turban and dark robes they wear. Most of the Druze are in Israel, some are in northern Jordan and southern Syria. Though Arab by descent, they hold themselves aloof and have a history of rebellion and struggle for independence under the various rulers in the Middle East.

369

*366/367. Two pastoral views at the Horns of Hittin.*
*368. The Horns of Hittin.*
*369/370. Druze shrine of Nebi Shu'eib, assumed to be the burial place of Jethro.*

370

Tabgha is the local corruption of the old Greek name *Heptapegon*, meaning seven springs. It was here, in this idyllic setting, that Jesus performed the miracles of the loaves and the fishes. "And he commanded the multitude to sit down on the grass, and took the five loaves, and the two fishes, and looking up to heaven, he blessed and brake, and gave the loaves to his disciples, and the disciples to the multitude. And they did all eat, and were filled: and they took up of the fragments that remained twelve baskets full. And they that had eaten were about five thousand men, besides women and children" (Matt. 14:19-21).

This miracle is commemorated in an exquisite mosaic that was part of the Church of the Multiplication, a Byzantine structure that was destroyed in the 7th century by the invading Persians or Arabs. One of the most beautiful mosaic floors in the Holy Land, it depicted a landscape with papyrus, lotus, flowering oleander, geese and flamingoes catching snakes, and a variety of decorative motifs, inspired by the flora and fauna of the region. The workmanship is of the highest quality, and suggests that it was done by one of the prominent artists of the period. A new church was built on top of the old one, to protect the mosaic.

Nearby is the Benedictine Hospice built by the German order in 1888, which nowadays is a youth hostel, run by the government. Set amid lovely gardens overlooking the lake, it is perhaps the most beautiful hostel in the land.

Near the Church of the Multiplications is the Chapel of the Primacy. It is also called St Peter's Church, in honour of the apostle to whom Jesus gave primacy over his other disciples, with the words: "Feed my lambs . . . feed my sheep" (John 21:15-16). In this chapel is kept a Crusader seal of the Galilee district, depicting Sts Peter and Andrew in a boat. This chapel, too, was built by the Franciscans over the ruins of an earlier one.

The area around Tabgha is one of the loveliest in the Holy Land. The warm climate and well-watered rich soil make for lush vegetation, including date palms, bananas and even pineapples. The lake abounds in fish, and cattle thrive in the fat water meadows. It is an ideal winter resort, especially for people who live in the much colder mountain regions, and so, for many generations, prosperous citizens of Jerusalem, Hebron and Safed would come here every winter.

*371/372. St. Peter's Church at Tabgha, also known as the Chapel of the Primacy, was built upon the rocks in the area Some of these can be seen here protruding inside the chapel.*
*373. This colourful peacock is part of the mosaic floor in the Church of the Multiplication.*

371

372

374

375

376

171

The Sermon on the Mount (Matt. 5-7) was given on what is called the Mount of Beatitudes, overlooking the north shore of the Sea of Galilee. From its summit, the landscape of the lake and its surroundings appears in all its serene and idyllic beauty. The words of the Sermon, full of hope and charity, belong in this setting: "Blessed are the poor in spirit, for theirs is the kingdom of heaven . . . Blessed are the meek, for they shall inherit the earth . . . Blessed are the peacemakers, for they shall be called the children of God . . . Love your enemies, bless them that curse you, do good to them that hate you, and pray for them which despitefully use you . . . Consider the lilies of the field, how they grow; they toil not, neither do they spin. And yet I say unto you, that even Solomon in all his glory was not arrayed like one of these . . . Judge not, that ye be not judged . . . Ask, and it shall be given unto you; seek, and ye shall find; knock, and it shall be opened unto you . . . Because strait is the gate and narrow is the way, which leadeth unto life, and few there be that find it . . .".

In the 4th century a church and a monastery were built at the foot of the Mount of Beatitudes, but these were destroyed by the Moslem conquerors in the early 7th century. The modern octagonal church on the summit of the Mount was built in 1937. Beside it a hostel and an Italian convent enjoy the exquisite setting.

*374/376. The Church of Beatitudes, adorned by the greenest of lawns and shrubbery, overlooks the Sea of Galilee.*
*375. Mosaic floor in the church.*
*377. View from the church to surrounding hills and lake.*
*378. An ancient gnarled tree in the grounds near the Lake.*

378

379

380

Hirbet Minya, like Hisham's palace near Jericho, was a fortified retreat of an Umayyad caliph. Lying on the northeastern shore of the Sea of Galilee, this was where Al-Walid I would rest from the bitter cold winters of Damascus, at the beginning of the 8th century AD.

Hirbet Minya was first excavated by archaeologists in the 1930s. They thought that the ruins were the remains of a Roman fortress, on account of the superb masonry. Later, the finding of gold Umayyad dinars, as well as parts of a mosque which was apparently never finished, and some medieval pottery, proved conclusively that this was the caliph's resort. It resembles the palace in Jericho and the hunting lodges on the sprawling tableland east of Amman in Jordan.

It is likely that although the owners were Moslem, some of the work was done by Greek Christian artisans and craftsmen, as suggested by the architectural and decorative details. Like all Umayyad fortresses in the provinces, the austere exterior masked a magnificent interior. Mosaic designs decorate the floor of the mosque; one mosaic floor, in a small room in the palace, resembles a carpet. Some of the towers and walls rise to almost 10 metres. In general, Hirbet Minya represents one of the best examples of early Moslem construction in the Holy Land, an architectural gem hidden under bramble-swathed rocks until the archaeologists uncovered it.

The remains here testify to the leisurely, elegant life led by these early caliphs. Escaping the rigours of the Syrian winter, they moved to the Holy Land, and spent their time hunting and basking in the sun.

The Greek Orthodox monastery of Capernaum stands on the shore of the Sea of Galilee, on the site of a church dedicated to St John the Theologian which had stood here during the Byzantine period. A small white building topped by red domes, its sunlit interior is furnished with Greek icons painted in a post-Byzantine style. Constructed in 1931, the monastery was vacant for a time, until 1967 when Greek monks again took up residence here. A few steps away from the building is a small landing, where boats are available for sailing on the lake.

*379/380. Remains of Hirbet Minya.*
*381. A monk and an old Greek woman are in charge at the monastery.*
*382. The Greek Orthodox monastery.*

381

382

An ancient village by the Sea of Galilee, Capernaum was mentioned by Josephus in his *Wars of the Jews*. In the New Testament it is described as the place where Jesus stayed on his sojourn by the Sea of Galilee, and Matthew (9:1) refers to it as Jesus' "own city". At least five of the apostles came from Capernaum and many of the miracles attributed to Jesus took place here.

"And when they were come to Capernaum, they that received tribute money came to Peter, and said: 'Doth not your master pay tribute?' He saith, 'Yes'. And when he was come into the house, Jesus prevented him, saying: 'What thinkest thou, Simon? Of whom do the kings of the earth take custom or tribute? Of their own children, or of strangers?' Peter saith to him: 'Of strangers'.

Jesus saith to him: 'Then the children are free. Notwithstanding, lest we should offend them, go thou to the sea and cast a hook, and take up the fish that first cometh up; and when thou hast opened his mouth, thou shalt find a piece of money. That take and give unto them for me and thee'" (Matt. 17:24-27).

In 1905 the remains of a synagogue were uncovered here and cleared and restored by the Franciscan fathers who are the custodians of the site. Dating from the late 2nd or early 3rd century, it is one of the best preserved Galilean synagogues of the early type. It consists of a main hall with one large and two small entrances in the façade which faces towards Jerusalem. Above the entrance is a large semicircular window with a sculptured frieze running around it. In the main hall there are two parallel rows of columns along its length and one transverse row, and stone benches along the walls. The interior is undecorated and there is no trace of a niche for the Torah ark. Steps outside the building led to an upper gallery, which is decorated with a stone frieze depicting

local plants, Jewish religious symbols — including the Tabernacles, *menorah* and Torah ark — and magic symbols such as the pentagram and hexagram. A colonnaded court with covered porches adjoining the building may have served as a guest house.

Above the main entrance there was a carving of an eagle with its wings outspread, and cupids bearing wreaths. These carvings were deliberately disfigured, probably by Jewish zealots in later periods, when the injunction against graven images began to be observed more strictly. Several of the beautiful friezes suffered a similar fate. Among the carvings that escaped mutilation is a handsome lintel decorated with two carved eagles bearing a wreath, and beside them a Capricorn (a fish-tailed goat-kid). There are also lions carved in the round, which had probably flanked the ark.

*383. Interior of the synagogue at Capernaum, one of the best-preserved of its kind. Its remains were uncovered at the beginning of the century.*
*384. Architrave ornamentation.*
*385/386. Embellished architraves and elaborately-designed capitals grace the synagogue columns.*

387

388

389

390

Two inscriptions found engraved on the columns read, "Alphaeus son of Zebedee wrought this column and blessed be he", and "Herod son of Mucimus and his son Justus with their sons built this column".

South of the synagogue traces have been found of the village to which the synagogue belonged. Their humble, unadorned forms, made of the local basalt, stand in contrast to the rather lavish house of worship. However, the village appears to have been well planned, with straight streets intersecting each other at straight angles. Also in this area was found an octagonal church, probably of the 5th or 6th century AD, with a splendid mosaic floor depicting a colourful peacock. The Franciscans, who uncovered it, believe that the church marked the house of St Peter.

From the Book of Ecclesiasticus we know that a Judaeo-Christian community existed in Capernaum in the Byzantine era. It was referred to in the Jewish sources as a sectarian community, which suggests that it was at least partly Christianized.

*387. Carving of cow head found at Capernaum.*
*388. Chariot of the Holy Covenant.*
*389. Palm trees in high relief.*
*390. Sculptured column base.*
*391. Detail of main entrance to Capernaum synagogue.*
*392/393. Sculptured architraves from the Chorazin synagogue.*

391

392

Some three kilometres from Capernaum, nestling in the hills of Lower Galilee, lie the ruins of the biblical town of Chorazin. It was a flourishing Jewish town in the period of the Second Temple, and the Talmud describes it as wheat-producing. When Jesus was preaching in the Galilee he came to Chorazin, but was disappointed by the lack of response he found there. "Then he began to upbraid the cities wherein most of his mighty works were done, because they repented not. 'Woe unto thee, Chorazin! Woe unto thee, Bethsaida! For if the mighty works which were done in you had been done in Tyre and Sidon, they would have repented long ago in sackcloth and ashes'" (Matt. 11:21-22).

The Church Father Eusebius, who lived in the Holy Land in the 4th century, described Chorazin as ruined, so perhaps it was destroyed at the time of the second Jewish revolt, in the 2nd century.

The ruined synagogue of Chorazin was also described by Peter Diaconus in the 12th century. This synagogue has been excavated and partially restored in this century. It is a magnificent and lavish structure, in the form of a basilica, built of basalt stones, with two rows of columns along its length and one row along its width. It is a large building — 24 by 17 metres in area, with a flight of stairs leading up to it. Its ornate façade faces south, towards Jerusalem. It is elaborately decorated with stone friezes depicting human beings and mythological figures, such as Hercules, a Medusa, a centaur and a variety of symbolic figures.

An interesting and significant feature that was found in the Chorazin synagogue is a seat carved out of a single basalt stone, in the form of an armchair. Its back is decorated with a rosette and on the front is an inscription in Judaeo-Aramaic naming a certain Judah,

son of Ishmael, as the builder of the colonnade and the staircase. The function of the seat is not known for certain, but it may have been a "seat of Moses", referred to in Matthew 23:2. This was presumably the place in which the scribe or some other learned person would sit to read aloud the Law.

The style of the decoration at Chorazin reflects the influence of Hellenistic culture on the Jewish community in Galilee. The capitals of the columns are both Doric and Ionic, with some modifications, and the carvings resemble sarcophagi and other stone ornamentations of the Hellenistic era in the Holy Land. There is nothing here of the abstract austerity traditionally associated with Jewish edifices.

One can easily imagine Jesus walking into the synagogue of Chorazin and preaching to its congregation. The soft hills and the balmy air of Galilee have not changed since those days.

393

394

Other than Jerusalem, there is no place that conjures up the Old Testament so much as does the Jordan River. Crossed by Jacob when he fled to his uncle in Padan Aram, crossed by him again when he returned to Canaan, accompanied by his wives and concubines, livestock and retinue, it was also the boundary between the desert and the Promised Land for Joshua and the Children of Israel when they came up from Egypt, going the long way around.

This slender line of silver that runs from the Sea of Galilee to the Dead Sea, lined on both sides with rich verdure and the sweetest meadows that can be found in this arid land, is also profoundly associated with the life of Jesus. Here Jesus came to be baptized by John, the forerunner, who called upon the people to purify themselves and to repent, for the Messiah was coming.

The Jordan is fed by the Sea of Galilee, which in turn is fed by underground streams and the snows of Lebanon. There are also a number of small tributaries, such as the Haron stream. Running, as it does, along the deep fissue of the Syrian-African rift, it is a sheltered, narrow valley, whose flora and fauna are unusually

395

rich and attractive. There are tropical and subtropical species here which are not found elsewhere in the region, and every year, spring and autumn, literally millions of birds stop for a rest beside the Jordan River, on their migrations between Europe and Africa. For most of its length, the Jordan River has not changed since the days when Jesus came down "from Galilee to Jordan unto John, to be baptized of him" (Matt. 3:13).

*394/396. The flora and fauna of the Jordan Valley.*
*395. Here Jacob crossed the Jordan.*
*397. The Jordan River at Almagor, where it flows into the Sea of Galilee.*

396

397

Two 12th-century Crusader castles overlook the Huleh Valley in Upper Galilee — on a mountain ridge east of Banias in the Golan stands Qalat Namrud, while, to the north, the fortress of Hunin lies on the edge of a steep cliff facing Mount Hermon. The latter, in fact, has been described by an Arab geographer as a "fort which stands on a single rock". Both castles were originally built to protect the vulnerable northern flank of the Crusader Kingdom. The importance of their location is proved by the historical fact that they were subject time after time to conquest and reconquest, that time and again they were razed to ruins, only to be magnificently restored.

Turning first to Hunin, which stands 675 metres above sea-level, overlooking the main route to Damascus, we find that it was originally called Castrum Novus (the New Castle) by the Christian knights who built it in 1106 under Hugh of St Omer, Crusader Prince of the Galilee. The fortress was taken 60 years later by Moslems, but not before the Franks had set it afire. The Sultan Nureddin did not set up residence at the site, as was customary, but rather had the castle evacuated and destroyed. Situated so close to other Frankish centres, the Sultan considered the fortress a poor choice for establishing a military base.

In 1178 Castrum Novus was recovered and rebuilt by the Crusaders, this time by Humphrey II. But the "old knight", as Humphrey was nicknamed, died in battle a year later and his restored fortress came under attack by Saladin. Only the determination of the Crusader defenders caused the Arab general to abandon his assault attempt. The castle then passed into the hands of Baldwin IV, King of Jerusalem.

Following the fateful Battle of Hittin in 1187, Hunin was one of three castles in the Galilee — along with Belvoir and Qalat Shaqif — to remain in Crusader hands. But the respite did not last; by the end of the year, after a five-month siege, it had fallen to al-'Adil, brother of Saladin. In 1222, for fear of its recapture by the Franks, the ruler of Damascus had the castle razed. The fortress again returned to the possession of the Franks in the middle of the 13th century under the terms of a peace treaty. In 1266 it fell to Baibars

and the Mamelukes, who rebuilt the castle and gave it its present name of Hunin.

Moving eastwards, one comes upon the Crusader fortress of Sebeibe or Qalat Namrud, named after the biblical Nimrod, the first "mighty one on earth" (Gen. 10:8), who is said to have been its legendary builder. Archaeologists, however, attribute the castle's origins to the Crusaders, who had it erected between 1130 and 1140. Its pattern of construction does not resemble other outposts of its type in the Holy Land. Taking advantage of the mountain's natural features, the builders of Qalat Namrud made it long and narrow — 450 metres in length and only 60 metres wide at one point.

Like Hunin, Qalat Namrud was continually subject to conquest. In 1164 it fell to Nureddin and thereafter followed a similar pattern of recovery and recapture. In the early 13th century the Sultan of Damascus had it destroyed, along with many other of the country's fortresses, including Hunin. Again it was Baibars who restored the castle and was the last to contribute to Qalat Namrud's construction. During the Mameluke period the fortress served as a prison before it was abandoned. In the 14th century it was razed by the Mongols.

The remains of Qalat Namrud which stand today provide a general outline of the original structure's uncommon shape. Part of the ruins indicate the former existence of a number of buildings whose purpose has not yet been ascertained. In the keep, at the extreme eastern edge of the fortress, Moslem wall paintings have

been discovered. Not far away, in the southern wall, stand the scant remains of the castle's main gate. Today the fortress can be approached from its western side, where a rock-cut moat protects the ramparts.

398. The Crusader fortress of Hunin. The snow-capped Mount Hermon is seen in the background.
399. Ruins of the southern wall of the 12th-century Crusader castle, Qalat Namrud. The archway was once the fortress' main gate.
400. Southern wall and tower of the Qalat Namrud fortress.

## THE SOURCES OF THE JORDAN

The Dan and the Banias are two of the main sources of the Jordan River. Both of these streams are associated with ancient cities that stood on their banks.

The Banias runs through lush woodlands, with oaks and fig trees and thick undergrowth, and ends in a broad lagoon, overlooked from afar by the snow-capped Mount Hermon. Beside the lagoon are some niches hewn out of the rock, remains of an ancient temple dedicated to goat-footed Pan, the god of all wild things. (The name Banias is the Arabic pronounciation of Panias.) Most of the temple was destroyed by an earthquake, but some of the inscriptions and traces of the paint on the walls remain.

During the period of Roman rule in the Holy Land, there was a city here, founded by Philip the Tetrarch, the son of Herod the Great, who named it Caesarion, in honour of Caesar Augustus. It became known as Caesarea Philippi, to distinguish it from the better-known city of Caesarea on the Mediterranean coast, and it is by this name that it appears in the New Testament: "And Jesus went out, and his disciples, into the towns of Caesarea Philippi, and by the way he asked his disciples, saying unto them; 'Whom do men say that I am?'" (Mark 8:27). The place is also mentioned in the Mishnah and Talmud.

In the year AD 70 games were held in this city to celebrate the triumph of Titus over Judaea, and many Jewish captives were killed on this occasion. It is difficult to-day, in the midst of this idyllic setting, to imagine the Roman city, its streets and arena, and the roar of the crowds. Rather, one fancies that the sweet pipes of Pan may

401

402

403

still be heard mingling with the murmur of the water.

Nearby Tell Dan is one of the few archaeological sites in the Holy Land which is shaded by trees and graced by running water.

According to the Book of Judges (Chapter 18), the tribe of Dan, which had its portion in the centre of the country, divided into two, one half migrating north and giving it its name. The tell is some 20 metres in height and includes buildings and fortifications from the Israelite era, starting with the 11th century BC. It was enlarged by King Jeroboam I, but was destroyed in the 9th century by Ben-Hadad, King of Damascus. It was later rebuilt.

*401. The source of the Banias.*
*402. The gushing waterfalls of Banias.*
*403. Rich overhanging foliage shades the Dan tributary.*
*404. Tiny pink blossoms grace the sky.*
*405. Roman designs and inscriptions carved in the rock at Banias.*

404

405

406

Rising out of a flat plain, guarding the Jordan River in the shadow of Mount Hermon, stands the largest tell in the Holy Land, Tell Hazor. Forty metres high, 600 long and 200 wide, it was a monumental challenge to the archaeologists, and one of the most rewarding excavations in the Middle East. Prof. Yigael Yadin, of Masada fame, headed the excavations of this tell in the 1950s. In the course of the digging, 22 levels were unearthed, reflecting every phase of its history.

The site of Hazor is, archaeologically speaking, unique. It is composed of two distinct parts, the tell itself and a huge rectangular plateau, to its north and east. The area of the tell itself is between 15 and 25 acres, which is not unusually large. The area of the plateau, however, is an incredible 200 acres, enclosed by a huge earthen rampart and defended by a deep and wide moat. For many years this was believed to be the site of a huge fortified camp, because it was difficult to imagine that it could have been a properly built-up city, considerably larger than Jerusalem in the days of King David. The exploration of the enclosure showed that it was indeed a city, and a magnificent one, in the Canaanite period, about the time of the Hebrew patriarchs. The later, Solomonic city and its successors, from the reign of Ahab on, were highly developed and sophisticated, with massive structures and elegant material culture, but were not as large as the original city.

In the Bible, Hazor is mentioned as one of Joshua's major conquests: "And Joshua at that time turned back, and took Hazor, and smote the king thereof, with the sword; for Hazor beforetime was the head of all those kingdoms . . . and he burnt Hazor with fire" (Josh. 11: 10-11).

These events took place in the second half of the 13th century BC. The evidence of the conflagration was plain in the thirteenth level of the 22 that were explored. This shows that Hazor was already

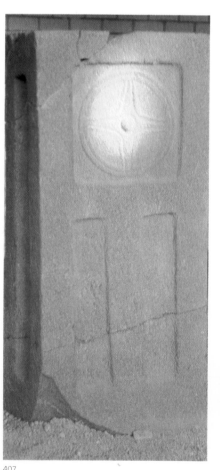

407

408

old at the time when the Israelites were sweeping across Canaan. In the Middle Bronze Age Hazor was the regular habitation of semi-nomadic people. During the New Kingdom of Egypt, Hazor was repeatedly mentioned in Egyptian texts as one of the kingdoms of Canaan. It was also known to the Mesopotamian rulers, as its mention in the Mari documents shows.

Even the earliest of the cities found in the enclosure was impressive for its town-planning and the sewage system in its houses. A sewage canal was found with an outlet hewn in basalt. When floors in this city were removed, to ascertain if it was indeed the earliest one, a large number of jars were discovered lying in the virgin soil. These were found to contain the skeletons of infants. The old idea that such finds represent a practice of child sacrifice has long been discarded, and archaeologists believe that, during the Middle Bronze period, infants were buried under the floors of their parents' home.

In the stratum that corresponds with the 14th century BC was found a small temple with basalt steles and statuettes. A central stele depicts two hands raised towards a semicircle, probably a half-moon, engraved into the surface. Also found in that level were a pottery cult mask and a silver-plated bronze standard bearing a relief of a snake goddess. At the northern end of the city the archaeologists found

*406. Restored vase dating from the late Bronze Age (15th-13th centuries BC), on display at Hazor Museum.*
*407. Stele from holy of holies of Canaanite temple found in lower city at Hazor.*
*408. View of Mount Hermon from Tell Hazor.*
*409/410. Excavation areas at the tell.*

409

410

411

four temples superimposed upon one another. Various cult objects were discovered here, such as a clay model of a liver, inscribed in Akkadian, and a bronze plaque showing a Canaanite priest draped in a long robe. These and various other finds indicate that Canaanite Hazor was a substantial city, fortified for much of its history, with palaces and temples and even underground drains. A fascinating find from the Israelite period is a potsherd with an incomplete inscription in proto-Sinaitic script — the precursor of the Hebrew alphabet.

The Solomonic Hazor was impressive, too. The city was refortified and had towers flanking its gate. Later it was destroyed by fire, and rebuilt again by the rulers of the House of Omri — the Kingdom of Israel, as distinct from the Kingdom of Judaea.

In the days of King Jeroboam II, an earthquake destroyed Hazor. This was the earthquake mentioned in the Book of Amos. The last fortified city at Hazor was destroyed by the Assyrians when they conquered the Holy Land and devastated the Kingdom of Israel. The most recent stratum dates from the Hellenistic period, about the 2nd century BC.

*411. A basalt vessel with Mycenean-style spiral carvings found at Hazor.*
*412. Remains of buildings in the vicinity of the Israelite citadel.*
*413. Tomb of Rabbi Yohanan Ha-Sandelar, who came from Alexandria in the 2nd century AD.*
*414. View of the synagogue at Meron.*

412

187

Rising 1,208 metres above sea-level, Mount Meron is the highest mountain in the Galilee, and second only to Mount Hermon. Bare and uninhabited, the mountain sleeps for 11 months of the year, battered by the winds, baked by the sun and swept by the rain. Then, shortly after Passover, when spring is everywhere, the slopes are alive with grasses and brightened with anemones and cyclamens, people begin to arrive from all over the country, to pitch tents and booths around the mountain top. These are pious Jews who come here to celebrate the 23rd day of the *Omer*

413

414

415

(the harvest count from Passover to Pentecost). When the day arrives there are thousands of celebrants sitting around bonfires, singing and feasting. The celebration is in honour of Rabbi Simeon bar Yohai, a 2nd-century Talmudic sage who spent 12 years hiding on Mount Meron, after being sentenced to death by the Roman authorities. Tradition ascribes to Rabbi Simeon the authorship of the *Zohar*, a mystical Kabbalistic work which was undoubtedly written several centuries after his time. The reason for this attribution is obscure. One of the customs associated with this

416

417

418

feast is the first haircut that is
given to small boys by the ultra-
orthodox families at Meron.

Beside the tomb of Rabbi Simeon, there is also a ruined synagogue from the Byzantine period
on the mountain. Its handsome
façade still stands, stark and impressive, suggesting past splendour.

Archaeological excavations revealed that there was a prosperous
Jewish town around the synagogue.
It flourished from the period of the
Second Temple until the middle
of the 4th century AD. Among the
structures unearthed were two
two-storied houses, linked together
by a shared terrace. They also
shared a cellar, in which huge
storage jars filled with nuts, grain
and beans were kept. Also found
in these residential structures were
various objects, such as silver
brooches, knives and spoons, elegant glass trays, and a small bronze
bell.

*415/416. Remains of the 2nd century
synagogue at Meron.*
*417. Tomb of Rabbi Simeon bar Yohai.*
*418. Worshipper absorbed in prayer.*
*419. Tomb of Eliezer, the Sage's son.*

419

The town of Safed is one of the most picturesque in the Holy Land. Clinging to a mountain top 850 metres high, in the Upper Galilee, it has a breathtaking view of Mount Meron, the Sea of Galilee and the rich, cultivated lands of the Lower Galilee, spreading like a precious carpet below the mountain range. Cool and breezy in summer, Safed is very cold in winter, buffeted by fierce winds, rain and snow-storms. Its small stone houses, separated by winding alleys and staircases, are a favourite haunt of artists, who have established a colony in the town which attracts tourists and art lovers from everywhere.

But today's peaceable aspect of Safed belies its stormy history. Although considered by the Jews to be one of the four holy cities in the land, it is not mentioned in the Bible, and makes its first appearance in the Talmud, where it is listed as one of the places where bonfires were lighted to signal the appearance of the new moon. It was probably one of the cities that were fortified by Josephus in the great Jewish war against the Romans. But from that time until the high Middle Ages there is no mention of Safed.

In the 12th century the Crusader King Fulk of Anjou built a tremen-

dous fortress in Safed, which dominated the region. Some years later King Amalric I of Jerusalem gave the castle to the Knights Templar, that order of religious warriors which controlled several important fortresses in the Holy Land. After defeating the Crusader forces at the Horns of Hittin, Saladin seized Safed, which thereafter changed hands several times, while the fortunes of the Crusaders rose and fell: dismantled by Saladin's successors, the fortress was rebuilt by the Templars in the 13th century, only to be recaptured by Baibars in 1266. This Mameluke Sultan strengthened the fortifi-

cations of Safed and made it the centre of the province of Upper Galilee and Lebanon.

Under Mameluke rule Safed flourished, becoming known for its spices, fruit and oil. At the end of the 15th century Jews from Spain made a considerable addition to the Jewish community of Safed. Having been expelled from Spain, these talented people spread around the Mediterranean, bringing with them the fruits of the great civilization of medieval Spain, with its intermingling of Latin, Arab and Jewish cultures. In Safed the newcomers were to write an important chapter in the history of mystical philosophy, enlarging the scope of the Kabbalah, which subsequently had a profound influence on such Renaissance figures as Pico della Mirandola and Johannes Reuchlin. This body of Jewish mysticism originated in ancient times, and during the Middle Ages reached Europe and North Africa. Here, in the tiny town of Safed, a brilliant and charismatic Sephardic Jew, Isaac Luria, created a new centre for the study of Kabbalah, and stamped it with his special spiritual quality.

When in the early 16th century the Holy Land passed into the hands of the Ottoman Turkish rulers, Safed benefited from the change. It was the administrative centre of a large region, comprising nearly 300 villages. To its traditional trade in spices, fruit and oil, was now added the more sophisticated industry of silk weaving, introduced by the Spanish

*420. A quarter of Safed seen from a higher part of the town.*
*421. Ha-Ari Synagogue at Safed.*
*422. Corner of the cemetery at Safed with the tomb of Rabbi Isaac Luria, who was known as Ha-Ari.*

421

422

423

424

Jews, whose products were said to compete with those of Europe. In 1563 a Jewish family by name of Ashkenazi established a printing press in Safed — the very first in the Orient. It was a period of growth and prosperity. However, in the 17th century the Ottoman rule in the Holy Land began to decline —its formerly energetic administration became lax and the province suffered as a result. Taxes, however, remained very high, while the economy declined, and the population began to dwindle. Constant warfare among the Beduin tribes of the Galilee, and periodic raids by these nomadic marauders, made living in Safed precarious. In the 1730s Ibrahim Pasha's rule, though benevolent, was marked by outbreaks of war between Arabs and Druze and finally an Arab revolt against the ruler. As if to compound the problem, first an epidemic and then an earthquake ravaged the town in the 18th century, and further reduced its population. Towards the end of the 18th century, however, a more efficient local government in the Galilee managed to bring about some improvement. Also at this time the beginning of Jewish immigration from central and eastern Europe increased the popula-

425

tion and infused new blood into the community. Thus, in the early decades of the 19th century things seemed to be progressing favourably for the little town in the mountains, until in 1837 a violent earthquake nearly wiped it off the face of the earth. Five thousand people, most of them Jews, were reportedly killed and almost all the houses destroyed. The blow left Safed reeling, and it hardly recovered until towards the end of the 19th century, when a number of light industries, schools and small farms gradually began to be introduced, thereby improving the living conditions for the existing population of Safed and slowly attracting newcomers.

Nowadays, Safed is one of the quietest and most attractive towns in the Holy Land. In the summer it is filled with visitors, who come up to enjoy its cool rarefied air, to get away from the heat and humidity which prevail in the coastal region.

The old quarters of Safed are still inhabited by deeply religious Jews who follow in the footsteps of the great Kabbalists, studying the hidden meanings of the Scriptures and the many texts written about them by former generations. There is a quarter known as that of the Old Kabbalists, where you can see synagogues associated with the memory of Isaac Luria.

*423. The Ten Commandments on the upper part of the Ark of the Law in the Ashkenazi Ha-Ari synagogue.*
*424. The Ark of the Law in the synagogue named after Rabbi Joseph Caro.*
*425. Studying the Law in a corner of the synagogue reserved for this purpose.*
*426. Ceiling of the synagogue named after Rabbi Isaac Aboab.*
*427. Interior of the synagogue.*

426

427

195

Gamla comes from *gamal*, the Hebrew word for camel, because this mountain, east of the Sea of Galilee, is shaped like a camel's hump. According to Josephus, it was here that thousands of Jews leaped to their death rather than face capture by the Romans during the great Jewish war in the 1st century AD. Excavations here have uncovered one of the earliest synagogues in the Holy Land.

Throughout the centuries of dispersion, from the AD 70 destruction of the Temple to the regathering of the exiles in the 20th century, there was always a Jewish community in the small village of Peki'in in the Galilee. It succeeded in retaining its ancient identity through Christian and Moslem eras. Rabbi Simeon bar Yohai and his son lived for 13 years in a cave near Peki'in, hiding from their Roman persecutors. Various Jewish antiquities from the Roman epoch have been found here. Also at Peki'in is the tomb of Rabbi Osayah of Tiria, an important talmudic sage.

*428. The fortress of Gamla.*
*429. The Holy Ark carved on a stone found at Peki'in.*
*430. Christian symbols above a gate.*
*431/432. Simeon bar Yohai lived in this cave, and ate the fruit of this tree.*

430

431

429

432

433

The synagogue in Bar Am, situated on a mountain top in Upper Galilee, is not mentioned in any of the ancient sources. It is, nevertheless, one of the best-preserved and one of the most beautiful ancient synagogues in the Holy Land. There were once two synagogues in the town of Bar Am,

suggesting that it had a considerable Jewish community during the early centuries of this era. In the 13th century a certain Rabbi Samuel ben Simeon passed this way, and wrote that there were two synagogues here, the smaller one being outside the town. Nothing remains of that structure,

except a lintel which is kept at the Louvre in Paris, which bears the inscription: "Let there be peace in this place and in all places of Israel".

The surviving synagogue is credited to Rabbi Simeon bar Yohai. It was described by Rabbi Moses Basula in the 16th century, and by the late 19th century by many other travellers and explorers.

The structure measures 15.2 by 20 metres. Its magnificent façade is preserved almost whole, with all the door and window openings, up to the upper cornice. There are indications that there were originally two stories, but nothing remains of the upper one. Like all synagogues, its Ark wall faces Jerusalem — in this case, southwards — but, unlike most synagogues, it has a porch along the entire length of its southern façade, supported by eight pillars. Giant ashlars, similar to the ones used in the construction of the

434                                    435

Temple Mount in Jerusalem, and in the Machpelah in Hebron, were used in building the Bar Am synagogue. The structure has three entrances — a large doorway in the middle, with a smaller one on either side of it. A low lintel over the main entrance was originally decorated with two winged figures, resembling the Greek goddess Nike, bearing wreaths. These were deliberately mutilated in ancient times, presumably by Jewish zealots. Above the lintel there is a frieze of a vine issuing from an amphora (a classical Greek vase, narrow at the neck and base, and having two handles). The two side entrances resemble the main portal in design. On the sill of the eastern window there is a carved inscription in Hebrew, "Built by Eleazar son of Yudan".

The area around Bar Am is one of the loveliest in the Holy Land, and is rich in historical associations. Sasa, mentioned in the Talmud as a town of the Sages, is a little south of here. Nearby, the Arab village of Jish is identified with the Hebrew Gush Halav, in Latin Giscala, described in the Mishnah as a "fortified city since

the time of Joshua". During the revolt against Rome in the 1st century AD, Gush Halav held out longer than any other Galilean Jewish town. The rebel leader, John of Giscala, was a native of Gush Halav. In the 2nd century Jews once again settled in this place, and there is evidence of a Jewish

community in the Middle Ages. Today it is an Arab village, largely Christian.

*433. Detail of main synagogue entranceway at Bar Am.*
*434. Pillars flank the entrance.*
*435. Façade of the synagogue.*
*436. Detail from the synagogue façade.*
*437. Maronite caretaker of the church.*
*438. Entrance to the Maronite church.*

The Galilean city of Kedesh numbered among the many conquests of Joshua and the Israelites in the land of Canaan (Josh. 12:22). The territory was allocated to the Levites and has also been cited as a city of refuge and as a fortified land belonging to the tribe of Naphtali (Josh. 20:7, 19:37). Some scholars associate this ancient site with a city mentioned in the list of lands conquered by Pharaoh Thutmosis III and also referred to in the El Amarna letters, but no conclusive evidence has turned up to support this theory.

In the 8th century BC the Hebrew city of Kedesh was captured and its inhabitants driven out by the Assyrians under Tiglath Pileser III. Yet Kedesh continued to exist in the Second Temple period in the territory of Tyre, as demonstrated by the remains of a Roman temple and mausoleum discovered at Tel Qadis, 25 kilometres north of Safed.

*439. Flowers on Naphtali Mountains.*
*440. Ruins of Roman sun temple at Kedesh.*
*441/442. Interior of Judin.*
*443. View to the north from archers' embrasure in castle.*

439

440

The Crusader castle of Judin was built in the 12th century for the specific purpose of guarding the city of Acre from the east. St Jean d'Acre, as it was called in medieval times, was a principal and strategically-located port — and thus a vital stronghold of the Christian knights. It was conquered by Saladin in 1187 and, following its recapture four years later by the English Crusader, Richard Coeur de Lion, castles such as Montfort and Judin were erected in its defence and farmsteads were established to ensure a steady food supply. The latter fortress and its surrounding land eventually came under the control of the Teutonic Knights.

The remains of Crusader Judin provide a sketchy outline of the original fortress, whose exact date of construction has not been determined. The castle was already in ruins in 1283, when the traveller Burchard visited it. Still visible today are a series of vaults in the southwest as well as the foundations of a tower to the east.

The restoration of Judin Castle was undertaken in the 18th century by the Beduin sheikh, Dahir al-Omar. Dahir was one of the pashas hired by the Ottoman sultans — who preferred to rule through local potentates — to raise a private army and collect taxes in the western part of the Galilee. During his rule, the sheikh welcomed Christian and Jewish settlers into his domain, in which the Judin fortress played an important part. In fact, the castle served him in his inevitable clash with the Turks for having overstepped his conceded authority and extended his control into parts of Samaria and northern Galilee. His ultimate defeat led to the abandonment of the restored castle, which is part of the fortress complex still standing to this day.

The fortress of Judin was again put to use much later in history by a group of Jews who founded the kibbutz of Yehi'am alongside the castle (hence the structure's present name — Yehi'am-Judin).

441

442

443

Of all the Crusader fortresses crowning the mountains of Galilee, the castle of Montfort is the most beautiful. Located 23 kilometres east of the seaside resort of Nahariya, the fortress is protected by steep cliffs on three sides, and its southern flank is defended by a moat. Originally a modest structure erected by the Frankish Crusaders, Montfort was later enlarged and made into a great castle by the Teutonic Order of St Mary. It was probably the centre of an agricultural community, as the fortress controls no strategic land routes. In addition, Roman coins and an urn, uncovered in excavations in 1926, indicate that the site had already been settled in antiquity.

In 1187 the castle of Montfort was destroyed by Saladin, to be rebuilt by the Hospitaller Knights in 1229. Today its ruins overlook a deep gorge and the narrow stream known as Nahal Chesiv in Hebrew, and Wadi Koren in Arabic. The site may be approached on foot by means of a small wooden bridge, following a three-kilometre hike through lush woods dotted with sturdy oaks. Much of the structure's original beauty is still visible; one of the first things that strikes the eye is the prominent 18-metres-high tower. One can also discern the remains of a main hall, two storage cellars, stables, cisterns and the church.

445

*444. The castle of Montfort set in a forest of greenery.*
*445. A closer look at the area's natural beauty.*
*446. Herd of cattle in the valley below.*

444

446

447

The bay of Acre, one of the finest natural harbours in the world, has served seafarers since ancient times. Assigned to the portion of the tribe of Asher, it was never actually ruled by the Israelites, remaining for many centuries a Phoenician port city. Its history is as dramatic and violent as any of the cities of the Holy Land. It was successive-ly conquered and lost by the Assyrians and Persians, and later by the armies of Alexander the Great, whose heirs ruled it for centuries. It was they who named it Ptolemais, and so it was called in the time of the Apostle Paul, who sailed from here. The Arabs renamed it Acre (Akko) and ruled it for centuries, until its conquest by Baldwin, the Crusader King of Jerusalem.

It was the Crusaders who gave the city the character we see to this day. They built it up on a grand scale, and fortified its port with the massive pile we see today, somnolent and yellow in the sun. There are grand halls connected by passages, and a splendid crypt, in honour of St John, which is supported by three massive columns. Some historians believe that it was not used as a crypt, but as a dining hall of the Crusading knights.

When Saladin's Saracen troops were sweeping the land they also conquered Acre, and held it until it was reconquered by Richard Coeur de Lion. Later it was again lost to the Moslems, and remained under Moslem rule until the 20th

448

century. Mamelukes and Turks gave the city the Oriental character we see today. They built the splendid mosque of Acre, one of the most magnificent in the Middle East, and an important religious centre. In one corner of the mosque, in a special green cage, are kept some of the hairs of the beard of the Prophet Mohammed, an object of profound veneration.

The courtyard of the great mosque is surrounded on three sides by elegant cloisters, featuring pointed arches and small domes. Behind them, the walls are decorated with exquisite faience tiles. Inside, however, the hall of the Moslem house of worship is very simple — its whitewashed walls are bare, except for some inscriptions from the Koran. Like

449

all mosques, this one has no benches or seats of any kind, and the worshippers kneel or sit on the floor.

During Ottoman rule Acre was a major port on the eastern coast of the Mediterranean, and caravans would converge here from all around the region. To accommodate them, several *khans* — Turk-

ish-type inns — were built in Acre. Some of them still stand — great arcaded courtyards, empty

447. *General view of the port city of Acre.*
448. *Towards daybreak the outlines of lone fishermen can be seen on the dock.*
449. *View of the harbour wall at sunset.*
450. *Remains of the Crusader breakwater in the bay of Acre.*

450

451

453

452

454

455

today and echoing with memories of the great camel caravans that used to come here from Damascus and Transjordan. Of the three *khans* of Acre today, the one called Al Umdan is the best preserved. It has a square, golden tower in the middle of its courtyard. Here you may see fishermen drying and mending their nets, as they have been doing for untold centuries. There are seafood restaurants lining the port which serve fish straight from the sea.

The Ottoman Empire was already in decline when Napoleon tried to seize Acre. He had swept up the shore of Palestine from Egypt, but here he was halted. The ancient port city, under its ruthless ruler Ahmed Pasha, withstood the French siege and, in fact, it was this reverse which marked the end of Napoleon's Middle East venture.

Ahmad Pasha's ruthlessness earned him the nickname *Al Jazzar*, the butcher. The city of Acre owes a great deal to this Ottoman ruler of the Galilee, despite his harsh personality. It was he who refortified the port city and built its superb mosque, named after him. Many of the public buildings that were constructed under his guidance, and which still stand, incorporate hewn stones which were transferred to Acre from the abandoned Roman and Byzantine ruins of Caesarea and Athlit.

The British Government, which ruled the Holy Land between 1919 and 1948, put the old Crusader fort to use as a prison.

In modern times the port of Acre lost its importance, as the harbour of Haifa, on the southern side of the bay, was developed and expanded, and eventually became the principal port of the Holy Land. Acre is still a fishermen's port, and a very attractive tourist resort, but its heyday is over. It is difficult to imagine, as you wander about the sunny courtyards, or along the great ramparts that overlook the sparkling sea, how many wars raged here, how many generals and princes fought over this city, subdued it and lost it. It seems eternally peaceful, a perfect image of a Mediterranean port.

*451. The courtyard of the mosque of Ahmad Pasha Al Jazzar at Acre.*
*452. Al Umdan khan at Acre.*
*453. Detail of wall-tiles at the mosque.*
*454. Twelfth-century ceramic fragments.*
*455. The caretaker of the mosque.*
*456. Carved stone architectural details.*
*457. Entrance to "St John's Crypt".*
*458. Ottoman aqueduct at Acre.*

458

456

457

One of the oldest cities in the Holy Land, Nazareth has a history going back some 3,000 years. But the fame of this small town, perched in the hills above the Valley of Jezreel, lies in its association with the life of Jesus. "And in the sixth month the Angel Gabriel was sent from God unto a city of Galilee, named Nazareth, to a virgin espoused to a man whose name was Joseph, of the House of David; and the virgin's name was Mary . . ." (Luke 1:26-28). Jesus was born in Bethlehem, in Judaea, but it was in Nazareth that he grew up and began to preach.

Nazareth today is not so very different from the small town that Jesus knew. The view of the Valley of Jezreel still spreads below the town like a variegated carpet, drowsy in the sun. In the narrow, winding streets of the old part of the city the cobblers and carpenters, tailors and bakers ply their trades as they have for many centuries. The sounds and the smells are not much changed. Despite its world-wide fame, Nazareth remains small, rural, absorbed in itself. The souvenir shops and tourist hotels cannot alter the special atmosphere of the place.

In the 4th century the first church was built on the site believed to be that of the Annunciation. It was a Byzantine structure, which was later enlarged, but was destroyed by the Persian invaders in 615. Under Arab rule the site remained in ruins, but when the Crusaders, led by Tancred, seized Nazareth in 1099, they proceeded to build a Romanesque church over the grotto and the ruins of the earlier structures. Tancred, who was titled Prince of Galilee, made Nazareth his capital. It did not enjoy much peace in the decades to come. Conquered by Saladin in

1187, it was recaptured by the Crusaders, led by Richard Coeur de Lion, in the early 13th century. In 1263 the church was destroyed by Baibars, the Mameluke leader, and was not rebuilt until modern times.

In the 18th century the Ottoman Turkish government allowed Spanish pilgrims to build a small church on the site. It was called Casa Nova. In 1799 Napoleon visited Nazareth and stayed at Casa Nova. Throughout the 19th century Franciscan fathers and other Christian religious orders helped to develop the little town.

The Basilica of the Annunciation was begun by the Catholic Church in 1955, and took ten years to complete. This was not a simple construction project — it entailed archaeological excavations that had to be conducted simultaneously with the building process. The Basilica as we see it does not stand on the ruins of the earlier churches, but rather over them, incorporating as much as could be uncovered and restored. It is a remarkable blend of modern architectural style with painstaking preservation of ancient and medieval structures.

The lowest level of the Basilica is that of the grotto, and the other ruined churches. Beside the staircase leading to the next level there is a set of six mosaic works depicting the 1964 visit of Pope Paul VI to the Holy Land. The church itself is on the next level, and it is brilliant with works of art from all over the world. Though the themes are all religious, taken from the New Testament, the styles vary greatly, from traditional-academic to abstract. Here, as in the great Romanesque and Gothic churches

of the past eras, the art is contemporary with the church, and combines religious expression with aesthetic appeal.

One mosaic picture, donated by African governments, depicts a dark-skinned Mary and Jesus receiving the offerings of African people,

*459. Colourful ceramic wares on show in a Nazareth shop.*
*460. Dome of the Basilica of the Annunciation in Nazareth.*
*461. The impressive façade of the Basilica of the Annunciation, decorated with Latin inscriptions and deeply carved figures. The tall, narrow design of the doorways and windows creates an illusion of great height.*

460

461

462

463

recalling the prophecy of Zephaniah: "From beyond the rivers of Ethiopia, even the daughter of my dispersed, shall bring mine offering" (3:10).

Another brillant mosaic from Japan shows a Virgin and Child with oriental features, in a garden of peonies. The artist, Luca Hasegawa, used cultivated pearl and gold inlay for Mary's robe. The American artist, C.L. Madden, contributed a metal sculpture of Jesus affixed to an abstract painting. A mosaic work by the Mexican José Garcia has the look of a watercolour painting, achieved by means of uneven pieces of the same hue. Fourteen ceramic reliefs, the work of Angelo Biancini of Italy, mark the Stations of the Cross. The stained-glass windows are of modern design, and the doors are covered with biblical scenes in bronze and embossed copper.

The baptistery, next to the church, is also an impressive artistic edifice. Built on an irregular octagonal floor plan, it is the work of Bernhard Hartmann and Irma Rochelle of West Germany. Hartmann is responsible for the bronze statue of Jesus and John the Baptist, and his wife covered the interior with sumptuous green and gold mosaic.

464

About 1.5 kilometres further north from the Basilica of the Annunciation is the Greek Orthodox Basilica. Here, according to tradition, was the "Fountain of Mary" where the Angel Gabriel appeared to the Virgin. The ancient well, whose cool, fresh water still flows, is inside the church.

The large number of churches in Nazareth reflects not only the tremendous diversity of the Christian faith, but also of the Christian community in the Holy Land today. The 100,000 Christians are divided into no less than 35 denominations! In Nazareth, in addition to the churches mentioned, there are also churches and institutions of the Russian Orthodox, the Maronites, Syrians, Copts, Armenians and several Protestant churches. A Moslem minority lives peacefully with the Christian majority — all are Arab by descent — and worship at the mosques whose minarets are interspersed among the church steeples.

The new town of Upper Nazareth, rising on the hillside nearby, is largely Jewish. Begun in 1962, it is carefully-planned and modern in style.

The bazaar is near the basilica — a typical Middle Eastern *souk*, with all the odours that belong to it. St Joseph was a carpenter and a glance at the bazaar will show that even today Nazareth is very much

462. *Interior of the restored Church of the Annunciation at Nazareth.*
463. *Greek Orthodox church containing the "Fountain of Mary", a well traditionally believed to be the spot where Gabriel appeared before the Virgin.*
464. *Arab women sell their wares in the Nazareth souk.*
465. *Interior of the chapel of Mary's Well.*
466. *The well holds cool flowing water.*

465

466

a city of craftsmen, as it was in biblical times. On a weekday the shop-fronts are bright with colourful mats and rush baskets, earthenware pots, drums, and silver and copperware. The craftsmen work in small alcoves behind the shops. The most sought-after artisans here are the nuns of the Greek Orthodox Monastery of the Annunciation, who renovate old icons and paint new ones. Orders for these icons come in from all over the world, but priority is given to the small Greek Orthodox village churches in the Galilee region, whose sparsely-furnished interiors are in need of ornamentation. The sisters describe their work as a "constant spiritual pilgrimage of discovery and enrichment". These artists and craftsmen provide Nazareth with its rustic quality, despite the town's ever-increasing population and the continuous flow of pilgrims and tourists roaming along its narrow streets.

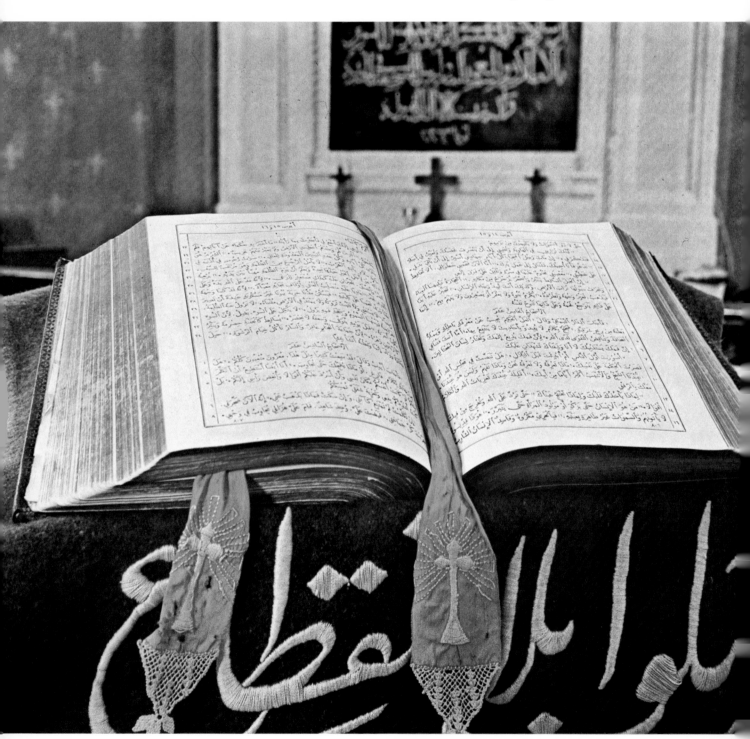

There are in Nazareth remains of a Jewish synagogue, perhaps the one mentioned in the New Testament, the place where Jesus preached his early sermons. One sermon so enraged the congregation that Jesus was driven from the town to be thrown off a cliff, which is located outside Nazareth — it is known as the Mount of the Leap.

The synagogue, essentially a fellowship of worshippers seeking God through prayer and study, gained in importance during the centuries following the destruction of the Temple of Jerusalem.

The communal prayer practised in the synagogue was later adopted by Christians and Moslems in their respective houses of worship. But in the time of Jesus the synagogue was the centre of religious and civic activity in Jewish communities outside Jerusalem and it was in this framework that Christ received his religious education, and found his first followers.

The remains of the synagogue may be seen inside a church. This area — near the bazaar and the Basilica of the Annunciation — is especially crowded with many houses of worship. What is left of the synagogue consists of 80 stones, some of which are inscribed and stuccoed, as well as some column bases. It is known simply as "The Synagogue", and is believed to date from the 6th century AD. Whether it was a synagogue in the modern sense of the word is open to question. Experts labelled it a Judaeo-Christian building, or a church built by the Byzantine Christians for use by Jews. One historian mentions a building which stood here in AD 570 and was originally a church converted into a synagogue. The site, which today is owned by the Greek Orthodox, was made into a chapel in the 18th century by the Franciscan Fathers.

The Nova Hospice serves Christian pilgrims who like to sojourn near the entrance to the bazaar, in the vicinity of all the churches.

The area around Nazareth is one of the most beautiful in the Galilee. It is surrounded by villages and ancient sites whose names are familiar from the Old and New Testaments. From the hilltops nearby, which were used as defence posts throughout history by Romans, Byzantines, Crusaders and Moslems, the landscape is much the same as it was in the lifetime of Jesus.

468

*467. The majority of the population of Nazareth is made up of Christian Arabs and the Old and New Testaments are read in Arabic. Here, the Bible in one of the churches is shown open at chapters 14-16 of the Book of Job.*
*468. The sign at the entrance to "The Synagogue" which is inside the Greek Catholic church and is believed to date back to the 6th century AD.*
*469. The door leading to "The Synagogue" which is now inside a church.*

469

470

It happened in his hometown of Nazareth, when Jesus was preaching in the synagogue. After he spoke for a while his hearers grew incensed at what they felt was his "presumption", for, they said, "Is not this Joseph's son?" (Luke 4:22). As the Gospel tells it, "all they in the synagogue, when they heard these things, were filled with wrath. And rose up, and thrust him out of the city, and led him unto the brow of the hill whereon their city was built, that they might cast him down headlong. But he passing through the midst of them went his way" (Luke 4:28-30).

"The brow of the hill", described in the Gospel, is about three kilometres south of present-day Naza-reth, and is known as the Mount of the Leap (*Saltus Domini*), or the Mount of Precipitation. Since there is a sharp drop of some 300 metres from its summit to the Jezreel Valley below, it fits the biblical description.

In Hebrew the hill in question is called *Har Kedumim*, meaning the Ancient Mountain. The name derives from some archaeological finds discovered in the place. The Franciscan fathers, who have custody over the local sanctuary, found a hidden cave with remarkable prehistoric remains. Excavations were carried out in the course of the 1930s. After digging through the medieval and Bronze Age levels, the archaeologists found ten strata from the Palaeolithic Age. In the highest one, they found part of a female skull and the jaw and forehead of a man. In the lowest stratum there were fragmentary remains of seven individuals.

Anthropologists disagree about these remains. Some believe that they are of Neanderthal Man, who inhabited these parts and whose remains have also been found in the Carmel. Others believe that they are earlier still. In any event, we know that early man lived in the hills around Nazareth 100,000 or even as much as 500,000 years ago. Compared with such vast lengths of time, our historical era seems brief indeed, and the day when Jesus was hounded out of town by the Nazarenes seems not much further back than yesterday.

*470. The Mount of the Leap, south of Nazareth, 300 metres above the Jezreel Valley. The Gospel tells how the enraged townspeople threatened to cast Jesus over its edge.*

*471. Giant cactus at Sepphoris*

471

Sepphoris (in Hebrew, *Zippori*) is first mentioned in the historical sources in connection with the reign of the Hasmonaean King Alexander Jannaeus (about 100 BC), when it was the administrative capital of Galilee. After the death of Herod the Great, the town was sacked by the Roman general Varus, and its inhabitants sold into slavery. It was rebuilt by Herod Antipas, who made it his royal seat for several years.

During the first Jewish revolt against Rome, Sepphoris did not resist the Roman legion, but rather enabled Vespasian to subjugate Galilee. In later years Sepphoris was the seat of the Jewish Patriarchate and the Sanhedrin. It also had a Christian community, and under Byzantine rule was the seat of a bishopric. For Christians the special association with Sepphoris lies in the fact that the Virgin's mother, Anne, came from this city.

Sepphoris was a considerable urban centre in the early Middle Ages. It contained two big markets, had many food shops and its measures were the standard for the Galilee district. It had paved streets and drainage installations, as well as a long aqueduct.

When the Crusaders arrived in the Galilee in 1099, they built the church of St Anne, and later a citadel. The town, which they called La Sephorie, guarded the road from Acre to Nazareth and Tiberias. It was from here that the Crusaders marched to the fateful battle against Saladin at the Horns of Hittin in 1187.

In the 18th century the castle of La Sephorie was refortified by Zahir al-Amr, who was at war with Jazzar Pasha of Acre.

472

The site of ancient Sepphoris was excavated in the 1930s, revealing a Roman building under the Crusader fort, a mosaic-paved basilica which might have been either a church or a synagogue, a theatre and an olive press.

The gaunt remains of the fortress stand on top of a hill commanding a fine view of Galilee. It is easy to imagine the Frankish knights, in their magnificent panoply in front of the greying stone pile, holding chivalrous meets, tilting and jousting under the enamel-blue sky of Galilee.

*472. The 18th-century castle fortified by Zahir al-Amr.*
*473. Lower corner of the fortress remains at Sepphoris.*

473

Here in this quiet little Galilean village, Jesus performed his first miracle. A poor family was holding a marriage feast, "and both Jesus was called, and his disciples, to the marriage. And when they wanted wine, the mother of Jesus saith unto him, 'They have no wine'. . .". Jesus bade the men draw water in waterpots, and "the ruler of the feast tasted the water that was made wine and knew not whence it was" (John 2:3-9).

The miracle has been celebrated in innumerable paintings and other works of art, most of them showing the place as very sumptuous,

rather on a Roman scale. In reality, Cana has not changed much through the centuries; today it is a tiny Arab village called *Kafr Kana*. It was conclusively identified as the biblical Cana by Quaresmius in the 17th century and, since then, churches have been built there and the place included in the itineraries of pilgrims.

The miracle is commemorated in two small churches. One is a Greek Orthodox church, which boasts two jars supposedly used by Jesus. There is also a Franciscan church in the centre of the village. It stands on the remains of a 4th-

474

475

century synagogue. This church also has an old jar, believed to be a replica of the one used in the miracle. The chapel adjoining the Franciscan church is named after St Nathanael because it stands on the site of the house of Nathanael of Cana, one of the disciples. It was he who wondered "Can there any good thing come out of Nazareth?" and later, when he met Jesus, exclaimed "Rabbi, thou art the Son of God, thou art the King of Israel!" (John 1:46,49)

In some subtle way, this quiet little village in its rural green setting, so remote from the world, seems to preserve the spirit of those times.

In his *Travels in Egypt and the Holy Land*, William Wilson, the 19th-century explorer, described his visit to Kafr Kana in these words: "Under the overpowering sun, I stopped at a fountain near the entrance of this village, to take refreshment. I sat down near the shattered well which inclosed it, and turned to that interesting passage of the Scripture, which records that six waterpots of stone were used at the nuptial feast, and the modest water saw its God and blushed . . .". He goes on to relate

how, just as he was reading this passage, six veiled women came down to the well to draw water, each carrying a stoneware waterpot on her head . . .

474. Catholic church of Kafr Kana.
475/479. The two churches at Cana.
476. Pottery found on the site.
477. Detail of Catholic church façade.
478. Interior of Catholic church.

476

477

478

479

480

There is hardly a more beautiful, breathtaking view of northern Israel than the one seen from the summit of the dome-shaped Mount Tabor. It was here that Deborah and Barak led the northern tribes of Israel in a victory over the armies of Sisera. Here, too, a Jewish stronghold withstood the Roman legions in the 1st century AD.

The peak of Mount Tabor is perhaps most renowned as the traditional site of the Transfiguration of Christ, where Jesus miraculously appeared to his disciples in the company of Moses and Elijah. In

481

tribute to its holiness, a Byzantine basilica was erected on the mountain top. The church was destroyed in the 7th century, rebuilt by the Crusaders and again razed by the Mamelukes in the 13th century.

The present basilica standing atop Mount Tabor was built in 1921 by the Franciscans (a Franciscan monastery is situated nearby). In the church garden can be seen ruins of the earlier structures. The interior of the chapel is of awe-inspiring beauty. Behind the altar, a glass mosaic ornaments the communion room. In the apse is a striking mosaic illustrating the transfiguration, with Jesus bedecked in white against a glittering gold background, his disciples looking on in wonder. Near the Franciscan basilica is the Greek Orthodox Church of Elias (Elijah).

This church is characteristic of many small Greek Orthodox chapels and churches in the eastern Mediterranean. Its walls bright with many icons, but otherwise, boasts little gold work or costly adornment. Set in a green meadow, it looks like a rustic church in a fairy tale.

*480. Gateway atop Mount Tabor.*
*481. The outline of the dome-shaped mount is distinguishable on the horizon*
*482. Mosaic of the Transfiguration in the apse of the Franciscan church.*
*483. Stained-glass window behind altar.*
*484. Façade of the Franciscan basilica.*

482

483

484

Though the name Afula does not appear in the Bible, some associate the site with the story of the Aramaean, Naaman, who was cured of leprosy by the Prophet Elisha (II Kgs. 5). Others speculate that it might have been a town which was destroyed during the reign of King Saul.

Archaeologists who excavated the nearby tell, have discovered remains dating as far back as the Early Bronze Age, and as late as the Roman Empire.

*485/486. Wall of Arab fortress at Afula. A number of sarcophagi were used in its construction.*

485

486

Megiddo, in the western part of
the Jezreel Valley, is the Armageddon of the New Testament — it is
here that the forces of good will
battle the forces of evil and win
their final victory (Rev. 16:16).
But aside from the eschatological
character attributed to it, Megiddo
is important in its own right, with
a history stretching back 6,000
years to Neolithic times. The site's
continued significance might be
explained by its location. Like
Hazor and Beth-Shean, ancient

487. *The main gate at Megiddo.*
488. *View over Canaanite altar onto
the Jezreel Valley.*

487

488

489

490

491

Megiddo dominated a vital pass. Situated along the route connecting Egypt and Mesopotamia, it controlled the territory between the coast and the Jezreel Valley.

The tell at Megiddo, first excavated by Israeli archaeologists in 1950, has revealed no less than 20 different strata, some of which may be further subdivided. The total figure reaches 25 levels and the most recent period was that of the Persian occupation in 500 BC. Archaeological finds here have partially verified certain biblical allusions to the site. For example, it seems that, like so many other places in this region of the Holy Land, Megiddo was a Canaanite city later occupied by the Hyksos and conquered by Joshua.

Under King Saul the ancient city fell to the Philistines. It was rebuilt, along with Gezer and Hazor, by King Solomon. Meant for his soldiers, Solomon had a strong casement wall built there, as well as a palace. Remnants of both were discovered by the German explorer and archaeologist, Gottlieb Schumacher, at the beginning of this century. Also attributed to the period of Solomon's rule is an elaborate water installation and tunnel system leading to a hidden spring at the base of the tell. And finally, construction of the famous stables for the 492 horses of Ahab, the Israelite King of Samaria, was probably begun at Megiddo at this time.

*489. Vegetation at Megiddo.*
*490. This altar, found at Tell Megiddo, dates from the Canaanite period.*
*491. Portico with pillars from the Solomonic period.*
*492. Remains of the famous stables of King Ahab at Megiddo.*
*493. Entrance to one of the structures uncovered at the tell.*

492

494

Outside of Jerusalem, there is probably no remnant of ancient Jewish civilization to compare with the ruins at Beth She'arim in the Lower Galilee. Spreading over an area of more than ten acres of mountain slopes, the ancient Jewish city flourished in late Roman times. An inscription discovered on the site confirmed the supposition that it corresponds to the town of Besara mentioned in the writings of Josephus.

The ancient community of Beth She'arim began in the 2nd century BC during the Hasmonaean period. Four hundred years later, the prominent rabbi and compiler of Jewish law, Judah ha-Nasi, made it the seat of the Sanhedrin, the assembly of scholars which served as the legislature and supreme court of the Jews. The rabbi is said to be buried in the town, which was also the home of many other Jewish sages whose words and deeds were cited in the Talmud. The city was destroyed in the 4th century following an ill-fated revolt against the Romans.

Beth She'arim is probably best known for its necropolis, dating from the 2nd to 4th centuries AD. Archaeological excavations have

495

unearthed an extensive system of catacombs, the largest containing 400 tombs. Of special interest is the rich ornamentation found throughout the underground structures. Tombs and sarcophagi are richly adorned with human and animal figures, as well as religious motifs (such as the seven-branched *menorah*). They lie along a number of corridors opening onto courtyards. The tunnels were dug out on a number of levels, their carving facilitated by the softness of the chalk rock. The tombs — some of which belonged to great families, but most of which were available for public use — are located in wall niches, also highly decorated; the bas-relief on one wall depicts the Holy Ark. The wealthy were buried in marble coffins ornamented by intricate friezes, indicative of a lenient interpretation of Jewish law, which forbids the carving of graven images. Inscriptions found on the sarcophagi — in Greek, Hebrew and Aramaic — indicate that many of the deceased were brought over

496

from Antioch, Beirut, Mesopotamia and even southern Arabia, testifying to the strong desire of the Jews to be buried in the Holy Land.

The decorations in the catacombs and on the sarcophagi are of great interest to historians and archaeologists, as they display the

evolution of Hellenistic influence

494. *Detail of tomb below.*
495. *Exterior of the tombs of Rabbis Simeon and Gamliel, talmudic sages.*
496. *Sarcophagus at Beth She'arim with animal figures as ornamentation.*
497. *The underground tunnels were carved out of the soft chalk rock.*
498. *Stone coffin with Hebrew inscription.*

499

in the Holy Land. Some of the ornamentation here is distinctly Grecian in inspiration — reliefs depicting Leda and the Swan, or Achilles in Scyrus, or a bearded figure reminiscent of a Greek god. Roman influence is seen in the style of funerary wreaths, bulls' heads and eagles. However, the vast majority of decorative motifs are traditionally Jewish symbols and ritual objects, executed in the rather naive style of the era. The two most popular motifs are the *menorah* (the seven-branched candelabrum of the Temple) and the Ark of the Law, complete with columns and steps. The ram's horn, palm-frond and *etrog* (the citrus fruit associated with the Feast of Tabernacles) are also used repeatedly. The stone doors — which still turn on their hinges — are decorated to look like wooden ones, with panels, nailheads and knockers . . .

Aside from the necropolis, five archaeological levels were identified on the site excavated at Beth She'arim. A large public building, whose basement and ground floor were studied, attests to the high standards of architecture practised in the area. Also discovered were the remnants of a 3rd-century synagogue converted into a Byzantine church. The ruins suggest a basilical structure, including three naves, and facing Jerusalem. The front courtyard was enclosed by three monumental gates. The ruins bear traces of Hellenistic influence and include columns topped by Corinthian-inspired capitals. Later, Hebrew and Greek inscriptions covered the walls. Interestingly, one of the Greek inscriptions bears the Hebrew word *shalom*. The synagogue appears to have been the largest in the Holy Land.

*499. Bas-relief of a Menorah held by a man clad in a Roman legionary's tunic.*
*500. Remains of a vaulted structure, belonging to the 3rd-century synagogue of Beth She'arim.*
*501. Group of worshippers praying outside the necropolis of Beth She'arim.*
*502. A rabbi at the entrance of the cave of the Prophet Elijah.*
*503. Worshippers light candles at the tomb of the Prophet.*
*504. Inside the cave.*

500

501

The Carmel range runs along the northernmost coastal plain of the Holy Land, and its majestic promontory over the Bay of Haifa made that part of the coastline famous among ancient seafarers.

The Phoenicians regarded the Carmel as the seat of the god Hadad, who was also called Baal of Carmel. In Roman times the oracle of Zeus of Carmel was consulted there. The Christian rulers of the Holy Land supplanted Zeus with St Elias, whom the Moslems called Al Khider. A monastery built on the Carmel in Crusader times was destroyed by the Moslems in 1291.

But one figure, revered by Jews, Christians and Moslems alike, is most closely associated with the Carmel, and that is the prophet Elijah.

There is a cave in the side of Mount Carmel, south of the city of Haifa, which is known as Elijah's cave and is considered a holy place by all three faiths. Here it is believed Elijah hid from the wrath of the Israelite king and queen. On the ridge above the cave stands the Carmelite monastery of Stella Maris — the Star of the Sea — which is a famous landmark of the Bay of Haifa. The inside of the grotto is lavishly decorated with an almost Byzantine opulence. A recess behind the cave is shown as the place where the prophet sat.

Elijah is sometimes described as the first monk — he was certainly a hermit for much of his life, but it seems to have been an outcome of his revolutionary activity rather than a deliberately chosen lifestyle. According to the Bible, Elijah did not die, but "went up by a whirlwind into heaven" (II Kings 2:11).

502

503

504

505

Halfway up the side of the Carmel, overlooking the city of Haifa, stands a white neo-classical building topped by a golden dome. It is the shrine of the Bahai religion, which originated in Persia in 1844, when a holy man who called himself Bab, meaning "the Gate", prophesied the ultimate spiritual unity of mankind. Driven out by persecution, the little sect of the Bab's disciples moved to the Holy Land.

In 1948, when the Jewish State came into being, the sect decided to make it the religious and administrative centre of its faith, and built their temple in the place where their prophet was buried. The gardens around it are exquisite, lending grace to the city of Haifa. Many Bahai believers visit the shrine each year, and the faith is officially recognized as one of the religions of the country.

*505-507. Bahai temple and library.*
*508. The horn of Carmel near Haifa.* -

506

507

There is a certain spur in the mountain range that overlooks the Bay of Haifa which is called the Horn of Carmel or, in Arabic, the *Muhraqa*. Here, in the reign of King Ahab of Israel, the Prophet Elijah challenged the priests of Baal to a contest to show whose god was supreme.

This was a difficult time in the Israelite kingdom. Ahab's wife, Jezebel, had introduced the worship of Baal and driven out, or put to the sword, the prophets of the Lord, except for 100 whom Obadiah, the King's major-domo, had hidden in a cave. Elijah, who was the scourge of the House of Omri, knew this, and knew too that he was feared and hated by the terrible queen. There was a bad drought that year, and consequently a famine in the land, and Elijah said to the people, "How long halt ye between two opinions? If the Lord be God, follow him, but if Baal, then follow him!" (I Kgs. 18:21). Establishing the rules of the contest, Elijah put the 450 prophets of Baal on the one hand, and himself on the other, each side preparing an altar with a dressed bullock on it, to see which of their sacrifices would be answered by God. The priests of Baal prayed to their god from morning until noon, and also "cried aloud, and cut themselves after their manner with knives and lancets, until the blood gushed out upon them" (28), but in vain. Elijah mocked them, saying that perhaps their god was away on a journey, or sleeping, and must be awakened . . . At last he himself prepared his altar, and drenched it with water, and then called upon the Lord of Abraham, Isaac and of Israel, saying: "Hear me, that this people may know that thou art the Lord God and

509

510

that thou hast turned their heart back again! Then the fire of the Lord fell, and consumed the burnt sacrifice, and the wood, and the stones, and the dust, and licked up the water..." (37-38). This was the end of the false prophets, whom the people pursued and destroyed entirely. And then "the heaven was black with cloud and wind, and there was a great rain" (45).

Some kilometres north of the *Muhraqa*, there is a Druze town by name of Daliyat al Carmel. Inhabited since the Middle Ages, its present population descends from some Druze clans who had moved down here in the 17th century. The events that led up to their settlement on the Carmel are one of the exciting and colourful stories of the Middle East. In 1590 a certain Druze leader, by the name of Fakr a-Din, rebelled against the Turkish Ottoman rulers of Syria and proclaimed himself Emir of Beirut. An energetic warrior and shrewd politician, he soon expanded his rule to include most of the Galilee, and later also northern Samaria and even Gaza. To strengthen his rule, he established several Druze villages on

512

511

229

the Carmel. Then he left the country to be ruled by his sons and spent a decade in Italy, where he studied the ways of the West. Despite rumours that he had converted to Christianity, and despite his prolonged absence, the Ottoman rulers of the Middle East were unable to overcome this small Druze emirate and subdue it. Gradually, however, they succeeded in inciting some of the local Arab leaders to rebel against Fakr a-Din's rule. The Beduin, too, were encouraged to ravage his territory. Fakr a-Din lost more and more of his emirate until, at last, disappointed by his Italian allies who had failed to come to his aid, he was defeated by the Ottoman forces in Safed. In 1635 he was beheaded in the Ottoman capital of Constantinople.

The Druze community on the Carmel declined after this setback. Despite several attempts to revolt against their oppressors, they never regained their freedom. Only in the late 19th century did their situation improve, when the Circassians — Moslems from the Caucasus — were settled in the Holy Land by the Turkish authorities, and the two communities supported each other against the Arab majority. Christian institutions, too, began to take an interest in the Druze people. The Christian mystic and early supporter of Zionism, Sir Lawrence Oliphant, lived in Daliyat al Carmel for a while.

Today the small town presents a pleasant, prosperous aspect. It is surrounded by prosperous fields and groves, and its inhabitants also make their living by working in small factories and workshops. There is a colourful bazaar in the centre of the town. The old men wear their traditional dress, a black robe with a white turban.

*509-512. Locally-produced items, ranging from woven baskets and brass-ware to cloth and hand-made rugs, are sold in the Druze village of Daliyat al Carmel, outside Haifa.*
*513. Statue of the Prophet Elias (Elijah) at* Muhraqa.
*514. Carmelite monastery at* Muhraqa, *dedicated to Elijah.*
*515. View of the Plain of Jezreel from the monastery.*

513

514

515

The customary association between the Beduin and the desert is not exclusive. Here, in the soft green landscape of the Galilee, these nomadic tribes have been pitching their tents for several generations. Originating from the Syrian and Transjordanian deserts, they came to the Galilee in the early years of this century, and have adapted their way of life accordingly.

*516/517. Beduin camp near* Muhraqa. *518/519. Walls of the Crusader fortress at Caesarea. The level earth in the bottom picture once served as a deep, water-filled moat.*

516

517

Caesarea is the epitome of a Mediterranean port city — a place where the sea and the rocks and the brilliant sunshine coalesce into a composition as old as time. There is an unchanging eternal tranquillity about the scene, underlying the pounding surf and blowing sea breezes.

Yet, for thousands of years this place was far from tranquil, far from the basic simplicity of sea and sun. As early as the 3rd century BC, the Phoenicians, those intrepid seafarers, built a port in this place, and named it Strato's Tower, in honour of one of their kings in

518

519

520

521

province, the harbour to those who sailed the seas, the honour of his new creation to Caesar. Caesarea was the name he gave it. The rest of the buildings — theatre, amphitheatre and market place — were on a scale worthy of that name" (Josephus, *The Wars of the Jews*).

The theatre mentioned by Josephus still stands, south of the main archaeological excavations. It has been restored and is used for the summer concerts of the annual Israel Music Festival. It is an experience to sit under the stars on a warm Mediterranean night, listening to great music against the sound of the surf and the sea breeze.

Herod built Caesarea in honour of his Roman protectors, in the style of their empire — which he admired and emulated. Ironically, it was here that the first outbursts of what became the first Jewish revolt took place. Tension had been building up for a long time between the Jewish community and the Syrian Greeks who formed the majority in the city. A clash in AD 66 led the Roman procurator of the province to intervene, with a resulting massacre in which, according to Josephus, 20,000 Jews were massacred within an hour. The response to this bloodbath was the great Jewish revolt against the Roman Empire.

As the capital of the Roman province of Judaea, Caesarea served as the headquarters of the Roman legions. The city was well-appointed and elegant, and offered the imperial officials some of the comforts of home. During Vespasian's stay in the city the legions stationed there rebelled and proclaimed him emperor. In gratitude, Vespasian later conferred the status of colony upon the city.

Sidon (today's Lebanon). About a hundred years later the town was conquered by a native tyrant named Zoilus. Next, it was the great Hasmonaean king, Alexander Jannaeus, who conquered the port city and incorporated it in his flourishing realm of Judaea. A Jewish community was established in the place and was thriving when Pompey came to the Holy Land and subdued it for the Roman Empire. Emperor Augustus gave

522

the city to his friend and protégé, Herod the Great, who renamed it Caesarea in his honour. Herod was one of the most ambitious builders of ancient times, and was responsible for some of the most grandiose structures of the age. He rebuilt the city of Caesarea and made it the largest port in the Holy Land. The Jewish historian Josephus knew Caesarea in its heyday and left a detailed description of it: "Herod dedicated the city to the

233

Archaeological exploration has revealed the magnificence of the city of Caesarea in ancient times. The Roman water-supply system was a tremendous one: beginning at the Zerqua River and the southern slopes of the Carmel, water was transported to the port city by a series of aqueducts. In the section near the Carmel it ran through a channel cut in the rock, and subsequently was carried through ceramic pipes resting on high arcades. The original structure dates from the reign of Herod. Damaged during the second Jewish war, it was repaired when Caesarea served as the headquarters of the Roman army. It is believed that the high-level aqueduct supplied drinking water to the inhabitants, whereas the second one, fed by the Zerqua River, was used to irrigate the surrounding fields.

Christianity became established in Caesarea as early as the 2nd century, when a bishop headed the community. In the 3rd and 4th centuries Origen and Eusebius, two of the Fathers of the Church, taught at the famous Christian school in Caesarea. From the library of this school came an early translation of the Bible known as the Hexapla. But life for the Christians of Caesarea was not much better than it had been for the Jews. There were persecutions and special taxes, directed especially against Christians and

Samaritans. There was also a large Jewish community, which at this time was no longer rebellious, having lost Jerusalem and political autonomy. Parts of the so-called Jerusalem — or Palestinian — Talmud were codified in Caesarea.

Under Byzantine rule the city was greatly adorned and embellished. New buildings were constructed on the remains of the Roman structures, such as a huge edifice which was built on top of

the Herodian podium. A citadel was built on top of the Roman theatre. A tomb containing gem-encrusted gold crosses dates the structure to Byzantine times. Remains of synagogues from that

520. A series of vaults grace the hall of the main gate of Crusader Caesarea.
521. Detail of vault with floral design.
522. Wall from Crusader period.
523. Cavities used for hitching horses.
524. Salamanders on the Crusader walls.
525. Series of stone archways at site.

523

524

525

526

period have also been found, identified by various Jewish religious symbols and inscriptions. It was also in this period that Caesarea was fortified by a new, circular wall, 2 kilometres long.

It was during the Byzantine era that Caesarea reached its greatest size and became the most important urban centre in the Holy Land.

An interesting structure from the Byzantine city was unearthed on a hill some distance east of the wall, on the other side of a cemetery. It could have been a church, but as no sign of a roof of any kind was discovered, it is surmised that the structure may have been built around an open courtyard and that funeral ceremonies were held there. It had a mosaic floor with a design of medallions enclosing various types of birds, surrounded by a border depicting sundry animals against a background of stylized fruit trees.

In the year 637 the Arab armies sweeping out of the east overwhelmed the country, and with it the port city of Caesarea. Under Moslem rule it lost much of its importance, being merely the capital of the district. The city declined. Only in the 12th century, under the rule of the Crusaders, did Caesarea revive again, if briefly. During the Sixth Crusade the port was fortified by Frederick II, and the ramparts were subsequently enlarged by the Crusader King of France, Louis IX.

527

528

529

These fortifications were uncovered in the early 1960s and today their golden masses dominate the archaeological site.

The Crusader city of Caesarea was actually the smallest, less than a sixth the size of its Roman or Byzantine predecessors. Its remains, which are by far the most substantial on the surface, include the wall with gates, a network of streets, a church, and the harbour fortress. The walls are impressive — the eastern one being 650 metres long, the northern and southern walls 275 metres each.

In 1265 Caesarea was reconquered by the Moslems, who devastated it as they did all the coastal cities — to prevent the Crusader armies from landing and seizing a foothold in the country. The ancient port city remained in ruins until the 20th century. The pillars lay in the water, sands blew and settled over the buildings, brackish swamps bred mosquitoes and attracted small predators. History seemed to have ended for the city of Caesar. Today there is a summer resort nearby, but the site itself remains quiet and uninhabited, if less wild, with nothing to suggest that it was the scene of so many dramatic and gory events.

The archaeological excavations at Caesarea have attracted many missions over the years. The first exploration was made by a British mission in 1873. In 1945 the British Mandatory Government's Department of Antiquities uncovered the remains of a synagogue floor. In the 1950s and 1960s more thorough excavations were made by Israeli teams, led by the late Professor Avi-Yonah. An Italian mission uncovered the Roman theatre in the years 1959-63.

*526. Capital embellished with menorah.*
*527. Roman aqueduct at Caesarea once used to carry water from the slopes of the Carmel.*
*528. Roman theatre used for concerts. In recent years large-scale opera performances have also been held here.*
*529. Roman statue found in Caesarea.*
*530. Inscription on rock slab.*
*531. Columns in the sea — ruins of the ancient port city.*
*532. The sparkling waters of the Mediterranean Sea at Caesarea's harbour.*

530

531

532

When Herod the Great founded a new city on the road from Jerusalem to Caesarea, he named it Antipatris in honour of his father Antipater. This had been an important junction since the time of Pharaoh Thutmosis III: it was the site of the Canaanite Aphek, which was conquered by Joshua and was where the Philistines forgathered before making war on Israel.

A fortress which had been built here in the Hellenistic period was conquered in the second half of the 2nd century BC by the Hasmonaean, John Hyrcanus I. The place was called Arethusa then, after the mythical huntress who was changed by a god into a natural spring. The name was particularly appropriate because there are many springs about the place. The town was rebuilt following Pompey's conquest of the Holy Land in 63 BC. But Herod, the most ambitious builder in the history of the Holy Land, built it anew.

Antipatris remained an important way-station for soldiers and travellers until the 4th century AD, but it was declining. Under Arab rule, in the Middle Ages, it again became important. The Crusaders built the castle of Le Toron aux Fontaines Sourdes at the site, now known as Tell Ras el-Ain; both names referring to the local springs. On the Crusader ruins, a square-shaped Turkish fortress was erected in the 17th century, the remains of which are still impressive.

*533. An aerial view of the fortress of Antipatris.*
*534. One of the finds at the site of Tell Kassila: an ancient water well with supporting stone columns.*

533

Some distance north of Jaffa, about 250 metres beyond the Yarkon River, rises a small hill which is known by the name of Tell Kassila. In the last three decades extensive archaeological excavations have shown this site to be one of the most interesting for the study of the Early Iron Age in the Holy Land. Though the ancient name of the town is not known, it is evident that it was an important urban centre throughout antiquity, especially in its Philistine period. The most recent finds date back to the Memeluke period, (15th century AD), but these are minor and insignificant.

The city was probably founded in the 12th century BC by the Sea People, who brought with them arts and crafts reminiscent of ancient Mycenae. In the third Philistine stratum (10th century BC), the city flourished, and its remains are most impressive. It was pre-planned, with parallel streets dividing rectangular blocks of buildings. There were special premises for oil presses, store-rooms and furnaces. There were local industries of copper-casting and dyeing.

Several temples dating from the Philistine period have been found, of which the best preserved is from the 10th century BC.

The city later belonged to the Israelite Kingdom, and an interesting Hebrew inscription on an ostracon from that period says: "Gold of Ophir to Beth Horon . . . thirty shekels". The abundance of small objects found on the site — including seals, scarabs, vessels, iron implements and pottery cult figures — helped to shed light on the culture of the Philistine, of whom little was known.

535

536

In the year 1909 a group of Jewish residents of Jaffa decided to build a new suburb north of the ancient port city, which was too densely populated and largely decrepit. They purchased some land — all of it rolling sand-dunes — and began to plan a small, modern garden city. Within a few years the new township, named Tel Aviv ("Spring Hill"), was showing all the signs of outgrowing its mother Jaffa. Sprawling over the golden sands, facing the blue Mediterranean, it soon boasted a good school — the Herzlia *gymnasium*, European-style — as well as a theatre, an orchestra, parks and . . . unlimited ambition! Broad, tree-shaded avenues ran down to the sea, a promenade lined with terrace cafés and family

537

# 239 TEL AVIV

hotels faced the beach, and neighbourhood after neighbourhood sprang up, consisting mostly of small residences or modest apartment houses.

Tel Aviv, known as "the first Hebrew city", became the heart of Jewish Palestine. The Hebrew press and book publishing became established here, as well as many of the social and cultural institutions of the Jewish community of Palestine. Other industries also grew up and developed on the outskirts of the new city, attracting a younger population. When the new port of Haifa pushed that of Jaffa into a secondary position, the ancient city declined and gradually became an exotic, if shabby appendage of Tel Aviv. *Habimah*, today Israel's national theatre, an opera house, a municipal museum and art galleries attracted many creative talents. A metropolitan character, far more dynamic and modern than that of Jerusalem or Haifa, made Tel Aviv the urban centre of the whole country. Its first colony rivalled that of Jerusalem, producing a style which reflected modern trends in the Western world. In a country preoccupied with its ancient history, Tel Aviv stood for novelty and modernity, being unencumbered with remains of older eras.

Today Tel Aviv sprawls over a vast area, including many small townships which it gradually swallowed up in process of expansion. It is a brisk, business-like city, with many fashionable avenues and high-rise buildings, a lively night-life and cultural activity. It lacks the grace of the older cities, whose slower pace and sense of historical continuity characterize the Holy Land. And yet, its Mediterranean climate, its hinterland of orange groves and prosperous farms are very much of this country, and no less characteristic than the traditional sites. It symbolizes the eternal youthfulness of the Holy Land, which has seen empires come and go, declined and rose again, vital and exciting as before.

*535/536. This synagogue was built in 1921, to serve Tel Aviv's old-age home. Its architectural style resembles that of East European synagogues.*

*537. A prosperous private residence characteristic of the architectural style of Tel Aviv in the 1920s and 1930s. The deep shady porches offered protection from the fierce sunlight.*

*538. This building, constructed in 1925, was Tel Aviv's Town Hall until 1965. Today it serves as the Museum of the History of Tel Aviv-Jaffa.*

538

539

Jaffa is popularly believed to be the oldest port in the world. It was certainly one of the very first ports on the eastern coast of the Mediterranean, which was the cradle of the earliest seafaring people. There are many legends and many historical events associated with this beautiful city that rises on a small promontory jutting out into the sea. One of the oldest legends is about the lovely Andromeda, the princess who was chained to a cliff, to be devoured by a sea-monster. She was rescued by Perseus, who turned the monster into a rock, which is still pointed out to visitors, basking in the sunny sea off Jaffa.

In the 12th century BC the Sea People, or Philistines, arrived and began to build cities all along the coast. The legend of Perseus and Andromeda may well have originated with them. Archaeological evidence suggests that Jaffa remained a Philistine city for a long time, and was not colonized by the Israelite tribes. In the centuries that followed, the important port city of Joppa, as it was called in Greek, was occupied by a succession of rulers, including Assyrians, Sidonians and the Hellenistic rulers of Egypt, the Ptolemies. During the wars of the Maccabees the city was burnt down in reprisal for the massacre of some 200 Jaffa Jews. Later it was conquered and annexed to the Hasmonaean kingdom. When Pom-

540

pey conquered the Holy Land he made Jaffa a free port city and it was ruled by a Syrian governor, but Julius Caesar returned it to the Kingdom of Judaea. Then Mark Antony gave it to Cleopatra, Queen of the Nile, but Augustus returned it to Herod . . .

The Apostle Peter, when he was in Jaffa, lodged with "one Simon, a tanner, whose house is by the sea side . . . Peter went up upon the house top to pray, about the sixth hour. And he became very hungry, and would have eaten, but while they made ready he fell into a trance" (Acts 10:6, 9-10). Then he had the vision that was to permit Christians to eat the flesh held unclean by the Jews. It was also in Jaffa that the woman disciple Tabitha (Dorcas) was resurrected by St Peter, and that the Apostle was commanded by the voice of God to bring the new faith to the gentiles as well as to the Jews.

Jaffa was destroyed by the Romans soon after the outbreak of the Jewish revolt, but was quickly rebuilt. The Jews kept a fleet of ships ready in the harbour in case of a renewed attack by the imperial forces, and when the troops sent by Vespasian against the city caught its defenders by surprise one night, they escaped into the ships. But a storm rose in the morning and dashed all the vessels against the rocks, killing most of the people on board. The survivors were massacred by the

541

542

*539. Part of the old port city of Jaffa overlooking the ancient harbour.*
*540. View of the dock of the old harbour of Jaffa.*
*541/542. Nowadays the port of Jaffa serves only light fishing boats. The old quarter that overlooks the sea is a popular artists' colony.*

543

544

545

543. *The minaret of the Sea Mosque at Jaffa.*
544. *The clock tower at Jaffa, built by the Turks in the 19th century.*
545. *Votive inscriptions on the fountain, built in the 19th century by Abu Nabbut, the Ottoman ruler of the town.*
546. *View of Jaffa where it joins Tel Aviv; the old harbour can be seen in the background.*
547. *The steeple and a corner of the façade of the Greek Orthodox church at Jaffa.*

546

548                549

550

Romans. All this is told by Josephus Flavius in his *Wars of the Jews.*

Jaffa was conquered by the Crusaders in 1099, before they reached Jerusalem. It was the principal gateway to the Holy Land, and was fortified by Emperor Frederick II. In 1268 it was conquered by the Mameluke Sultan Baibars, who razed it to the ground and massacred its population. Though rebuilt again, Jaffa's fortunes declined, and it was only in modern times that it regained its position as the principal port of the Holy Land, retaining it until the development of Haifa in the 20th century.

Today Jaffa is a beautiful old town, overlooking the blue sea, its charming alleys full of memories of the past, which blend with the sea breeze and the tempting odours that arise from the fish restaurants near the shore. Tel Aviv's southern neighbour, it is also the modern city's mother, and the favourite haunt of artists and tourists alike.

*548. The steeple of the Franciscan church of St Anthony at Jaffa.*
*549. A tower of a different style.*
*550/551. The church of St Peter built by the Franciscans, with their symbol on the doors.*
*552/555/556/558. Restored old houses.*
*553. The door of the old caravanserai.*
*554. The tomb of Abu Nabbut.*
*557. The house of Simon the Tanner.*

551

552

553

554

555

556

557

558

From the top of the tower of Ramlah there is a magnificent view of the plains between the Judaean Hills and the coast. This six-storey, 30 metres-high square tower, with 119 steps leading to the top, is a fine example of Islamic architecture, reminiscent of similar structures found in other parts of the great Islamic Empire.

The edifice was built in the 14th century by the Mameluke rulers of the Holy Land. It was designed to serve as a minaret for an adjacent mosque that had been built in the 8th century, when the Arabs founded the city of Ramlah (meaning Sandy) to serve as their capital in the Holy Land. It is known as the White Tower, or the Tower of the Forty Companions (of the Prophet).

Another square tower in Ramlah is at the Hospice of St Nicodemus. Owned by the Franciscan Order, it served as Napoleon's staff headquarters in 1799, when he was trying to wrest the country from the Ottoman Turks. Tradition has it that the French general directed the assault on Jaffa from the top of the white tower.

One of the oldest bridges in the Holy Land spans the narrow stream known as the Ayalon River. At its base are several rows of massive square hewn stones, dating back to Roman times. Its upper part was built by the Mameluke Sultan Baibars (late 13th century), as the long Arabic inscription over the pointed arch states. The inscription is flanked by two lions, Baibars' emblem, familiar from the Lions' Gate in the wall of the Old City of Jerusalem.

*559/560. The White Tower at Ramlah. 561/562. Bridge over Ayalon River at Lod with Baibars' heraldic device.*

561

562

Guarding an important junction, where the Judaean foothills rise from the coastal plain, Gezer was a strategic city in the Canaanite and Israelite eras. Archaeological excavations at the huge tell have uncovered a particularly rich hoard of inscriptions, including a 2nd-millennium BC potsherd in Proto-Sinaitic script, cuneiform tablets from the 7th century BC and the famous 10th-century BC "Gezer calendar", which is the earliest example of Hebrew writing.

The tell is famous for the Gezer High Place, 10 huge blocks of stone standing in an open space at the northern end of the mound. Some of these monoliths are more than three metres high. Archaeologists have dated the High Place to the middle of the Canaanite epoch, when part of the inner city wall was erected.

The outer wall, also found by the excavators, served the city throughout its history. The towers and other additions to it were built by King Solomon. In fact, the Iron Age saw repeated destructions and renovations in Gezer's fortifications. Pharaoh Sheshonk conquered the city in 918 BC, but it was not the first time that Egyptians defeated Gezer: in the 15th century BC, the city had been conquered by Thutmosis III. The Pharaoh slaughtered the Canaanite inhabitants, and gave the town to his daughter, whom he married to King Solomon.

Two centuries later, Gezer was conquered by the Assyrian armies of Tiglath-Pileser. Its subsequent history is obscure, except for a mention by Josephus of a Maccabean fortress in Gezer.

*563. The ten monoliths of the Canaanite High Place at Gezer.*
*564-567. Ruins at Modi'in, believed to be the burial-place of the Maccabees.*

249

Nestled in the Judaean foothills is an ancient village associated with the Jewish struggle for freedom in ancient times. Modi'in, now an Arab village, was the birthplace of the Maccabees, founders of the Hasmonaean dynasty. Here the patriarchal father of the family, Mattathias, launched the uprising against the tyrannical Seleucid Syrian king, Antiochus Epiphanes. (On the famous Madaba Map is written: "Modeim, which today is Moditta, wherefrom were the Maccabees".)

The year was 166 BC, Mattathias' sons with the eldest, Judah, at their head, led the Jews in a successful struggle to overthrow the Hellenistic empire whose centre was in Syria, and which tried to suppress the practice of Judaism. The tombs of the Maccabees were described by Josephus in the *Antiquities of the Jews*: "Simon also built a very great monument of polished white stone, and raised it to a great and conspicuous height, and erected monolithic pillars, a wonderful thing to see. In addition to these he built for his parents and his brothers seven pyramids, one for each, . . ." (XIII:211).

Unfortunately, though a few rock-cut tombs exist dating from the Hasmonaean period, it is not certain they are those of the Maccabees. Nothing remains of the monuments described by Josephus.

565

566

564

567

568

569

Emmaus lies on the eastern edge of the coastal plain, where the Judaean Hills begin their gradual ascent towards Jerusalem. Here the Maccabees won a great victory over the Seleucid Syrian forces, commanded by Gorgias and Nikanor, in 166 BC. The victory gave the Maccabees control of the western approaches to Judaea. After the great Jewish war in the 1st century, Emmaus became a Roman army camp.

On the Sunday after Jesus was crucified and buried in Jerusalem, two men journeyed from the Holy City to Emmaus. The Gospel according to St Luke tells how Cleopas and Simon, returning home during the day, encountered a stranger and offered him lodging for the night. The man accepted the offer of hospitality but disappeared immediately after. Realizing that this was the risen Jesus, the two men returned back to the Holy City, where the news of their encounter was spread.

The archaeological corroboration of the story began when a devout French noblewoman, the marchioness Pauline Nicolay, came to the Holy Land in 1861. She purchased a piece of land in Kubeibe, in a place she believed there was an "ancient room" connected in some way with the Gospel narrative. Later she moved to Jerusalem and the land was turned over to the Franciscan Order. Excavations on the spot revealed a Crusader church constructed over the remains of a Byzantine one, which, in turn, was built over an "ancient room", believed to be the house of Cleopas. It was later discovered that near the church was a Crusader village which straddled a Roman road leading to Jerusalem. This village consisted of one-room houses, some with adjoining courtyards. A wine press and large bakery were uncovered as well. Below the Crusader village are the remains of Byzantine and Roman settlements.

Archaeological evidence indicates that the village was built according to plan, all the houses being constructed at the same time. The Frankish settlers who occupied the place were driven out by Moslems at the end of the 12th century, and it was not resettled. In the following century, the Crusaders regained control of Emmaus as part of a peace treaty.

Sadly, Pauline Nicolay did not live to see archaeologists prove the soundness of her belief. She is buried inside a church constructed in 1901 on the ruins of the Crusader structure excavated on her land. In fact, the first few metres of the building's walls were erected by the Christian knights. Some of the Crusader stones were later used by the Turks to rebuild the walls of Jerusalem. What remains from the traditional house of Cleopas is enclosed in glass. The church is part of a fortified convent which was also a hostel for lepers.

Many scholars disagree with Kubeibe's identification as the New Testament Emmaus, believing it to be at Amwas, not far from Latrun, the site of the Maccabees' victory.

Kubeibe is also the site of an ancient synagogue used by the Samaritans. It testifies to the presence of a Samaritan community here in the late Roman period.

Gibeon, a few kilometres north-west of Jerusalem, was a great Canaanite city when the Israelites settled in the Holy Land. Joshua commanded the sun to stand still over Gibeon. Here, too, King David won a victory over the Philistines.

Though the history of the place dates from the Early Bronze Age, the archaeological remains are mostly from the Israelite epoch; they consist of fortifications, a rock-cut circular pool, tunnels, wine cellars, houses and inscriptions which helped to identify the site.

A spiral stairway leads down to the bottom of the 25 metre-deep pool which was probably used to store rainwater. It may have been the pool referred to by the prophets Samuel and Jeremiah (II Sam. 2:12-17, Jer. 41:12). Near-by are two tunnels which carried water from the underground source of a spring. One of them carried water from the pool to a point within the city itself. This tunnel is 50 metres long and, like the rest of the system, was probably constructed about the 10th century BC. This meant that Gibeon was assured a water supply during a siege.

The discovery of the wine cellars was preceded by the finding of jar handles, each stamped with the seal of the city. There were 11 such cellars, each about 2 metres deep. The openings were closed with giant stone slabs.

In later eras, the wine cellars were used as tombs or to store water. The Romans also dug a new reservoir north of the spring.

The area around Gibeon is dotted with many sites going back to the Early Bronze Age.

*568/569. Remains outside the house at Emmaus where Jesus met two of his disciples.*
*570. The spiral stairway leading down to the bottom of the pool, both cut in the rock, where water was stored at Gibeon.*

The foothills of the Judaean mountains, with their soft covering of trees and vineyards, are among the gentlest landscapes in the Holy Land. Here, near the western approach to Jerusalem, is a monastic compound whose inhabitants have taken a vow of silence so as to devote themselves to contemplation.

The monks who settled in Latrun in the late 19th century, belonged to an ascetic order founded at Soligny-la-Trappe, France, and are therefore known as Trappists. They drained the mosquito-breeding swamps in the area and began to cultivate the land. In 1927 they built the magnificent Italianate building which lends grace to the valley it overlooks. Here the monks study theology, work in the fields, and make wine from their vineyards.

Near the monastery are the remains of the 12th-century Crusader fortress, Le Toron des Chevaliers (Old French for "The Tower of the Knights"), from which Latrun gets its name. The name Le Toron was also confused with *latro*, the Latin word for "thief", since the place was called "the house of the good thief" by Christians who believed it to be the home of St Dimas, the thief who repented his sins before being crucified beside Jesus. The Crusaders settled the area in 1099 and built their fortress on the hilltop, possibly on the remains of an earlier structure that was part of ancient Nicopolis, a city many believe to be the Emmaus of the New Testament. After a battle that was fought here between Richard Coeur de Lion and Saladin, the Moslem forces captured

the fort. But it was to change hands a few more times before the structure was finally destroyed by Saladin.

In addition to a fortress, the Christian knights built a basilica on the ruins of a Byzantine church. That edifice was also damaged in the Middle Ages, and finally destroyed in the 19th century by the Egyptian Ibrahim Pasha.

Though Latrun today is a picture of perfect serenity, it was actually one of the most fought-over sites in the Holy Land, as the hill dominates the vital crossroads linking the highway from Jerusalem to Jaffa with the one going from Gaza and Ashkelon to the northern reaches of the Judaean Hills. Here in early biblical times Joshua battled the Canaanites and in the 2nd century BC the Maccabees fought the Seleucid empire of Syria during the early stage of their revolt. Supported by Hellenized Jews and pagans, the Syrians massed their forces here in preparation for an attack on the rebels. Before sunrise, part of the Syrian army left camp to surprise the rebels in their mountain strongholds. But Judah the Maccabee, using an alternate route, attacked Latrun from the rear while only part of the Syrian forces was there to defend it. The first contingent returned after dark without having located the rebels, only to be faced with the sight of their burning camp. The Maccabees then attacked this remaining Syrian army, and achieved complete control of the western approaches to Jerusalem.

In later times this was the site of a permanent Roman camp for the forces led by Titus during the

first Jewish rebellion. It was 68 AD, and the Roman commander was on his way to vanquish the Holy City. Inscribed gravestones in the vicinity of Latrun substantiate this tale.

After the crushing of the Jewish uprising and the destruction of the Second Temple, Latrun became a small Jewish town. When Bar Kokhba led the Jews in the second revolt, in the 2nd century AD, the people of Latrun aided him. The uprising failed, and Latrun was captured by the Romans. They later founded the city of Nicopolis on the ruins of the Jewish town, making it a district capital in the 3rd century AD. During the late-Roman and Byzantine periods both Jews and Samaritans lived here: archaeologists have uncovered a 3rd-century Samaritan synagogue and the remains of a 4th-6th-century church. The synagogue is especially interesting on account of its Greek and Hebrew inscriptions: "His name will be blessed forever" in Hebrew, and "God is one" in Greek.

It was also from Latrun that the British army launched its successful attack on Ottoman-Turkish Jerusalem in 1917. In 1948, Latrun was again the setting of fierce battles between Jewish and Arab forces.

Today, seeing the silent monks working in the lush vineyards, while nothing disturbs the tranquil air, it is difficult to imagine this hillside and the valley that stretches smilingly below as the scenes of terrible bloodshed.

*571. The Italian-style Trappist monastery overlooking the valley of Latrun. 572-575. Remains of the 12th century Crusader castle,* Le Toron des Chevaliers. *Here a battle was waged between Richard Coeur de Lion and Saladin.*

572

573

574

575

On the road leading from the coastal plain to Jerusalem lies the Arab village of Abu Ghosh. Its position gave it strategic importance and affected its history in dramatic ways. The Romans built a road through the village and a giant water cistern for the use of travellers. Over it the Crusaders built a church, when they were on their way to the Holy City. The fortress-like structure encloses the ancient well which still provides water for the thirsty visitor. The Romanesque church is part of a monastic compound run by French Benedictine monks. Underneath it are the remains of a Roman fort. It is one of the loveliest churches in the country; there is about it a quality of dynamic strength and a presence unmatched even by the Crusader castles in the Galilee.

The world inside the monastery is one of eerie silence, where giant pine trees brood and sway in the wind, creating a medieval European ambiance that the religious architecture enhances. Before entering the church one comes upon a stone sarcophagus containing the remains of an unknown warrior. Beside the entrance to the building there is an inscribed tablet stating that these grounds were once occupied by the Roman Tenth Legion. The remains of a *khan* (inn) from the medieval Moslem period are also in the vicinity.

A few kilometres further along the road to Jerusalem, there is a bubbling brook, screened by luxuriant undergrowth and hidden among oak trees. The Crusaders called it Aqua Bella, "Fair Water", and built a fortified farm nearby. There is a tradition that it was a nunnery — the Moslems call the place *Deir al Banat* "the House of Women" — but it seems unfounded. The 40-metre long walls contain a courtyard, a hall and the remains of a small tower. An outside staircase leads to the upper floor. All around are great old trees, and the place is an oasis of peace and beauty.

Aqua Bella is now surrounded by a national park, approached through a landscaped-meadow, bisected by the brook running into a series of rock-cut pools. The façade of Aqua Bella rises at the end of the meadow.

Near Abu Ghosh and Aqua Bella is Mount Castel, a strategic point 750-metres high, guarding the road to Jerusalem. Romans, Crusaders and later conquerors used it as a key outpost. It has been identified with the biblical Perez-Uzzah, where the Ark of the Lord fell off the cart while being taken to Jerusalem: "And David was displeased, because the Lord had made a breach upon Uzzah: and he called the name of the place Perez-Uzzah to this day" (II Sam. 6:8).

576

*576. Statue of the Virgin overlooking the village of Abu Gosh.*
*577. Seal of the Roman Legion on a stone incorporated by the Crusaders in the wall of the church.*
*578. Tomb in a niche near the church.*
*579. Entrance to the Crusader church.*
*580. Crusader structure at Aqua Bella.*

577

578

579

580

# Index

Abraham's Well 57
Abu Gosh 254
Acre 59, 202-204, 213
Adummim (Plain) 105
Afula 218
Aelia Capitolina (Jerusalem) 66
Al-Azariya see Bethany
Amram Pillars 42
Annunciation 16, 153, 207, 209
Antipatris (Caesarea) 236
Aqua Bella 254
Arabs 55, 71, 137, 152, 160, 168, 181, 192, 202, 209, 211, 234, 235, 252, 254
Arad 54, 55
Aravah 49
Arbel 165, 167
Armenians 20, 72, 91, 96, 97, 119, 209
Ascension (Church) 93
Ashkelon 58-62, 252
Atharim 54
Avdat (Obodah) 45, 48-53
Ayalon (River) 247
Bahais 226
Banias 180, 181, 183
Bar Am 196, 197
Beatitudes (Mt. of) 170, 171
Beduin 23-25, 36, 37, 46, 57, 96, 107, 199, 229, 230
Beersheba 56, 57
Belvoir (Castle) 152, 153
Benedictines 100, 168, 254
Bet Alfa 151
Bethany (Al-Azariya) 100, 119
Beth-El 57, 108, 109, 132, 143
Beth Guvrin 62-66
Bethlehem (Ephrath) 70-72, 77, 96, 119, 121, 206
Beth Shean 146-149
Beth Shearim 222-224
Beth Shemesh 66
Byzantine (period, style) 11, 13 15-17, 19, 35, 51, 53, 57-59, 74-77, 79, 90, 104, 105, 113, 115, 118, 123, 130, 133, 134, 148, 151, 165, 168, 173, 176, 189, 211, 217, 224, 225, 233, 235, 250-253
Caesarea 182, 230-236
Cana (Kafr Kana) 214, 215
Capernaum 173, 174-176
Carmel (Mt.) 30, 212, 226, 227, 235
Carmelite monastery 225, 229
Castel (Mt.) 254
Cave of Machpela 68, 69, 72, 73, 138, 197
Chesalon 83
Chorazin 177
Church, Casa Nova 207
Church(es), Greek Orthodox 209, 214, 242
Church, Maronite 197
Church of Abu Gosh 254
Church of All Nations 93
Church of Beatitudes 171
Church of Magdalene 93
Church of St Anna 62
Church of St Anthony 244
Church of St Catherine 13-17
Church of St Elias 217
Church of St George 49
Church of St John the Baptist 118
Church of St Lazarus 100, 101
Church of St Peter 157, 168, 244
Church of St Theodorus 53
Church of the Annunciation 207, 209, 211
Church of the Ascension 143
Church of the Holy Sepulchre 31, 90, 91, 166
Church of the Multiplication 168
Church of the Nativity 71-73, 119
Church of the Primacy 168
Copts 30, 31, 119, 209
Coral Island 45
Cross (Monastery of The) 93
Crusaders 20, 22, 41, 45, 59, 61, 62, 71, 75, 78, 89-101, 104, 109, 110, 130, 134, 137, 139, 152, 153, 157, 158, 166, 167, 180, 181, 190, 199, 201-203, 206, 207, 211, 213, 217, 225, 230-235, 244, 250-256
Daliyat al Carmel 228, 229
Dan (River) 57, 183
Dead Sea 57, 107, 121
Dead Sea Scrolls 89, 121, 178

Dome of the Rock 94
Druze 167, 192, 228, 229
Ebal (Mt.) 137, 143
Edom 45, 47, 69
Egypt, Egyptians 22, 30, 31, 38, 57, 62, 106, 119, 135, 138, 142, 147, 148, 152, 167, 185, 221, 248
Eilat 38, 45
Ein al Sultan (Spring of Elisha) 113
Ein Doch 113
Ein Fara 105
Ein Karem (Bet Hakerem) 84
Elah Valley 66
El Aqsa (Mosque) 94
El Maghtas 118, 119
Emmaus 250, 251
En Gedi (Fountain of the Kids) 122, 123
En Mishpat (Kadesh) 40
Eshtemoa 74-77
Ezion-Geber 45
Flagellation (Convent) 157
Franciscans 72, 84, 101, 157, 174, 207, 212, 215, 217, 244, 246
Galilee 74, 152-201
Galilee (Sea) 152, 154, 156-162, 164, 171-174, 178, 190, 195, 205, 210, 222, 228, 230, 254
Gamla 195
Gaza 41, 228, 252
Gennesaret (Kinneret) 158
Gerizim (Mt.) 137, 138, 140, 142, 143
Gethsemane 93
Gezer 248
Gibeon 251
Gilboa 152
Gilgal 57
Golan 74, 152, 158, 180
Golgotha 90
Gush Halav (Jish; Giscala) 197
Haifa 159, 225-227, 239
Hammath 151, 154, 155
Hathor 36
Hazor 184-186, 221
Hebron 54, 68, 69, 74, 138, 168, 197
Hellenistic 51, 55, 57, 63, 123, 133, 136, 143, 148, 177, 223, 224, 235, 240, 252
Hermon (Mt.) 158, 180-185, 187
Herodion 81-83
Hirbet al-Mafjir (palace) 116
Hirbet Minya 172, 173
Hittin (Horns of) 152, 159, 166, 167, 190
Holy Sepulchre 23, 31, 166
Hormah 55
Hunin (Castrum Novus) 180, 181
Jacob's Well 134-139, 178
Jaffa 59, 237-246, 252
Jericho 78, 100, 104-112, 119, 172
Jerusalem 66, 67, 70, 73, 78, 83, 85-100, 104-108, 118, 124, 136, 140, 166, 168, 174, 177, 178, 184, 222, 224, 239, 250, 251
Jezreel (Valley) 151, 206, 212, 219, 221, 229
Joppa (Jaffa) 240
Jordan (River) 106, 118, 119, 152, 156, 178, 179, 182-184
Joseph's (Patriarch) Tomb 138, 139
Judaea 47, 70, 74, 81, 83, 84, 89, 104-112, 118, 121, 123-124, 136, 182, 186, 232, 241, 245, 249, 250
Judin 198
Kadesh 40
Kadesh Barnea 41, 54
Kafr Kana (Cana) 214, 215
Kedesh 198
Kidron 78, 79
Kinnereth (Lake) see Galilee, Sea
Kornub 52
Kubeibe 250; see also Emmaus
Latrun 252, 253
Magdala 164
Majdal (Ashkelon) 61
Mamelukes 69, 95, 96, 104, 106, 130, 135, 181, 190, 191, 203, 207, 237, 246
Mampsis (or Mamshit) 52, 53
Mamre 68

Maon 41
Mareotis 31
Maresha 62-65
Mar (Saint) Saba 78, 79
Maronites 197, 209
Mary's Well 209
Masada 82, 124-129
Megiddo 219-221
Meron 186-190
Moab 106
Modi'in 248, 249
Monasteries:
    Abu Gosh 254
    Armenian 72
    A-Tor 33
    Bethany 100
    Capernaum 173
    Carmelite 225, 229
    Coptic 31
    El Maghtas 119
    Franciscan 72
    Greek Orthodox 20, 35, 93, 210
    Mar Saba 78, 79
    of the Cross 93
    of the Holy Trinity 119
    Quarantal 110
    St George 108, 109
    St Hariton 105, 110
    Trappist 252, 253
Montfort (Castle) 201
Muhraqa 227-230
Moslem shrines 34, 47, 105, 106, 133, 138, 225
Mosques 11, 41, 94, 95, 101, 106, 139, 203, 205, 242, 247
Mount Carmel 225
Mount Castel 254
Mount Ebal 137, 138, 143
Mount Gerizim 137, 140-143
Mount Hermon 158, 180-184
Mount Meron 187
Mount Moriah 94
Mount of Beatitudes 170, 171
Mount of Olives 91, 99, 100
Mount of Precipitation 212
Mount of the Leap 211, 212
Mount Scopus 84
Mount Sinai 10, 11, 26, 27, 34
Mount Tabor 16, 152, 216, 217
Mount, Temple 84, 94, 96, 106
Na'aran 114, 115
Nablus (Sechem) 131, 134-139, 143, 146
Nahal Arbel 165
Nahal Chesiv 201
Nahal David 123
Nativity 71-73, 119
Nazareth 206-213
Neapolis 41, 136, 137, 144
Nebi Musa 106, 107, 118
Nebi Salah 34, 37
Nebi Shu'eib 167
Negev 38, 40, 45, 48, 51, 54
Nile 22, 31, 33
Nirim (kibbutz) 41
Nureddin 181
Oases 23, 34, 35, 40, 41, 110, 112, 116
Omar (Mosque of) 95
Patriarches (tombs of the) 68, 69
Peki'in 194, 195
Perez-Uzzah see Mt Castel
Persians 49, 70, 71, 78, 98, 109, 110, 137, 168, 221, 225
Pope's Mosque (The) 101
Ptolemais (Acre) 202
Qalat Namrud (Nimrod; Subeibe) 181
Quarantal (Monastery of the Forty Days) 110
Qumran 121
Rachel's tomb 73
Ramallah 131
Ramlah 246
Red Sea 45
Rephidim 34
Romans 10, 53, 55, 57, 59, 61, 66, 67, 72, 83, 86, 113, 123, 124, 126, 133-137, 143-146, 148, 156, 158, 165, 172, 182, 195, 197, 198, 201, 213, 214, 216, 218, 222-225, 232-236, 241, 247, 250, 254
Russians 93, 100, 209
Sabil Qaitbay 95, 96
Safed 168, 190-193, 229
Saladin 139, 143, 152, 159, 166, 167, 190, 199-202, 206, 252

Samaria 130, 131, 134, 137-144, 228
Samaritans 134-138, 140-144, 199, 233, 250, 253
Samoa 74
Samson 41, 58
Santa Caterina (Monastery, Church— 11, 13, 17, 19, 22, 23, 24, 25, 26
Sasa 197
Sea Mosque 242
Sebastia 139, 146
Sepphoris 212, 213
Serabit el-Khadam (Pillars of the Slaves) 36, 37
Shechem (Nablus) 134-140, 143
Shiloh (Tell Seilun) 132, 133
Shivta (Sobota) 47-52
Shomron (Samaria) 144
Shrine of the Book 89
Sinai 10, 11, 14, 19, 23, 25-27, 36-38, 49 122, 130, 148, 186, 248
Solomon's Pillars 42
Solomon's Pools 77
St Anna 62
St Andrew 168
St Anthony 10, 31, 244
St Basil 22
St Catherine 11, 14, 20, 23
St Cyril 78
St Dima 252
St Elias 225
St George 108, 109
St Hariton 105, 110
St Jerome 72
St John Climacus 11
St John the Baptist 118, 119, 208
St John the Theologian 173
St Julian 157
St Lazarus 100, 101, 157
St Mari Mina 31
St Mary 84, 143, 157
St Nathanael 215
St Nicholas 79
St Nicodemus 246
St Peter 157, 168, 174, 176, 241, 244
St Saba 78
St Simeon 31
St Stephen 26, 27
Stella Maris (Monastery) 225
Susiya 74
Synagogues 41, 74-77, 87, 109, 113-115, 123, 129, 133, 143, 148-151, 157, 174, 175, 176, 186, 189, 191, 192, 196, 197, 209, 239, 250, 253
Syrians 20, 110, 165, 209, 228, 230, 232, 249, 250, 252
Tabgha 168
Tabor (Mt.) 16, 152
Tekoah 78
Tel Aviv 143, 238, 239, 244
Tell Afula 218
Tell al-Balata 135
Tell Dan 183
Tell Hazor 184
Tell Kassila 237
Tell Ras el Ain 236
Tell Seilun 132, 133
Temple Mount 84, 94, 96, 106, 197
Tiberias 151, 154, 155, 157, 158-163, 166, 195, 213
Timna Copper Mines 42
Transfiguration, The 14-16, 216, 217
Trappists 252, 253
Turks (Ottoman) 56, 59, 71, 97, 99, 104, 114, 118, 130, 159, 191, 199, 203, 205, 207, 228, 229, 236, 242, 246
Valley of the Inscriptions 38
Via Dolorosa 90, 91, 119
Wadi al Sheikh 34
Wadi Ariga 123
Wadi Firan 34, 35
Wadi Kelt 104, 105, 108, 109
Wadi Koren 201
Wadi Sidri 45
Wailing Wall (Western Wall) 87
Yad Vashem 88
Yavneh 162
Y.M.C.A. 98
Yad Mordechai 83
Zemah 159
Zerqa (River) 233
Zin (Desert) 46, 47

Shlomo S. Gafni

Text

A. van der Heyden

Photography

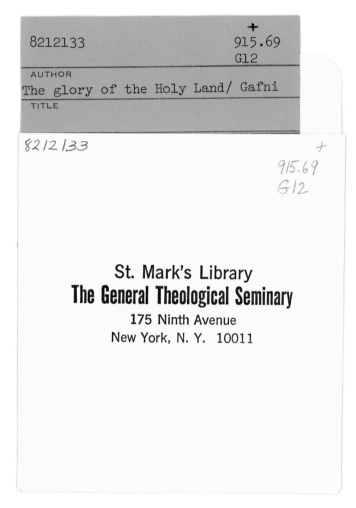
ADDITIONAL PHOTOGRAPHY:

A. Alon (No. 276); W. Braun (Nos. 534, 538); N. Drucker (Nos. 564-576); A. Hai (Nos. 333, 334, 342, 533); D. Harris (Nos. 60, 68, 179, 241, 242, 253, 267, 277, 278, 280, 284, 291, 321, 322, 325, 347, 379, 380, 400, 427, 447, 449, 450, 453, 454, 456, 457, 467, 526, 540); Israel Department of Antiquities and Museums (Nos. 274, 275 — exhibited in Rockefeller Museum; Nos. 331, 332, 526 — exhibited in Israel Museum); Palphot (Nos. 69, 260, 340, 341, 428); Photo Sadeh (No. 70); Z. Radovan (Nos. 59, 204, 206, 207, 211, 216, 220, 381, 382, 421, 535, 536, 537, 539, 541-558).